MYSTERIOUS DISCOURSES
Wisdom that Awakens the Heart

FATHER SIMON
the Hermit

Mysterious Discourses, Wisdom that Awakens the Heart © 2017 Fedor Beskrovnyy. All rights reserved. No part of this book may be used or reproduced in any manner whatsoever without written permission of the author, except in the case of brief quotations embodied in critical articles and reviews.

Translated from Russian by Dmitry Starostin.

First US Edition: August 2017
Edited by Maribeth Gray and Mark Savchuk.

ISBN: 978-0-9963389-4-3
Library of Congress Number: 2017952125

20 19 18 17 16   5 4 3 2 1

Cover and Interior Book Design

mysteriousdiscourses@gmail.com

Dedicated

To all the Wise Elders who are leading the way

and

To all those who follow.

Table of Contents

Introduction — vii

Chapter One: Looking for Salvation — 1

Chapter Two: Getting a Prayer — 25

Chapter Three: Heart Purification — 49

Chapter Four: Controlling the Mind — 75

Chapter Five: Mastering Thoughts — 101

Chapter Six: Silence of the Heart — 129

Chapter Seven: One with God — 155

Conclusion: Eternal Life — 179

Epilogue: Spring — 183

Introduction

The book that bears the title *Mysterious Discourses* can be appreciated by the thoughtful person of our time looking for answers to eternal questions: our purpose on earth, the meaning of suffering, the quest for God and the encounter with Him. *Mysterious Discourses* uses allegories and parables to convey the innermost spiritual realities that cannot easily be expressed in rational, modern language. They reveal simple and accessible wisdom, traditionally handed down by sages, so a reader can feel the deeper sense beyond the limits of the ordinary that has particular value and meaning. This book aims to awaken one's intuitive side and bring it back to life. It should also be noted that to truly understand allegories and parables, the reader's interest in co-creating a story is needed along with a desire to gain awareness and a transformed mind.

The constant activity of the mind, taken as the basis of reality, can be compared to watching TV which we sometimes do regularly accepting it as a glimpse of life. Watching TV, we cannot control the content, although we can change the channel. In the same way, there is the mind with its show that we watch constantly. We watch it in dreams at night and with our thoughts and emotions during the day. Watching this mind show, we control it even less than TV broadcasting. Usually, we do not even suspect how essential it could be to handle the mind to find answers to our eternal questions and to attain Wisdom.

In ancient, pre-Mongolian Russia, mind-focused teaching was wide spread. It came with Greek monks who practiced Hesychasm (silent contemplation) to Novgorod and Kiev in the 11th century. Later, in Moscow, this teaching was connected to Sergius of Radonezh, his follower, artist Andrei Rublev, and 15th century ascetics. Then Hesychasm decayed but was restored in the 18th century by Paisius Velichkovsky, who brought it back from Athos, Greece where it was known as "mind prayer"(Η νοερά προσευχή). Due to the Optina Elders and Valaam monks, which are two renowned Russian monasteries, the Hesychasm teaching, under the name "mind work" (Умное делание), became well known in 19th century Russia but was soon nearly lost in the Soviet Period. These monastic teachings, along with the required discipline, survived underground mostly in secluded areas in the mountains or in the territories added to the Soviet Union after WWII which were less influenced by atheistic propaganda and religious destruction.

Mysterious Discourses was conceived and written as a guide for spiritual life and encompasses the entire spiritual journey of the Orthodox Christian: from the earliest steps, the stage of the beginner or neophyte, to the uppermost step of perfection which is deification, assumption of God's nature.

The book was written by Father Simon, the Hermit, who was born in 1948 in the Russian Cossack village of Cuban and given the name Fedor Beskrovnyy. He became

Mysterious Discourses

a monk in 1986 at Trinity Lavra of Sergius, a Russian Orthodox monastery near Moscow. He took the name "Simon" with the guidance of their famous elder, Kyrill.

Later as a hermit, Father Simon spent long years in the Caucasus Mountains, in southern Russia, and then later moved to a small, secluded monastery on Mount Athos, Greece. He has written more than a dozen books on mind work published under his father's name, Monk Simeon. Some titles on religion and philosophy are: *About Divine Silence, Mundane Happiness and Heavenly Bliss, The Art of Fight with Thoughts*.

Father Simon, the Hermit, is liked and respected within the Orthodox community as noted by Metropolitan Nektarios (Antonopulos) of Argolida., a leader of the Greek Orthodox Church:

"In Russia, I met a modern ascetic... one I'd heard about from a friend from Trinity Lavra of St. Sergius who said, 'There is one, not so old monk, who has wished to follow the example of the great hermits of the desert. This is Father Simon...' The life of Father Simon has been full of adventures and finally he has chosen the Holy Mt. of Athos. All the fathers of Katunaki (an area on Mt. Athos) hold him in deep respect and I have heard only the best words about him."

And from Bishop Pankratius (Zherdev), the abbot of Valaam monastery:

"I spent a year in the Caucasus, with my friend, Father Simon, who later spent almost ten years there in the mountains in seclusion, writing wonderful spiritual poems. The Caucasian hermitages in Soviet times arose mainly because there were only four monasteries in the whole of the Soviet Union and it was necessary to go through big obstacles to get into them. Therefore, some people, aspiring to monasticism, went to the mountains of the Caucasus. Now he lives on Athos in Greece and is known as a spiritual writer."

The inner essence of the book is concealed behind the external and is aimed at overcoming the customary logical perception of spiritual categories and realities. The modern man lives more by reason than by the heart. So the intention of the innermost meaning is to awaken, to unravel in man the spiritual heart, the soul capable of perceiving spiritual tradition. Therefore, this book requires intuitive rather than intellectual reading. As soon as the reader feels that silent call to the depths of the heart, the comprehension of the innermost spiritual essence of the book will come by itself, step by step.

To conceive of the awareness and depth of spiritual life, it is valuable to read but more important to live in accordance with the words of the Scriptures. This book appeals to the Orthodox who try to realize the message of Christ in their hearts as well as anyone looking for eternal wisdom beyond the illusions of what we take as real.

> *"I thank thee, O Father, Lord of Heaven and Earth, because those hast hid these things from the wise and prudent, and hast revealed them unto babes."*
>
> St. Matthew 11:25

August 6, 2017   Mark Savchuk

Chapter One
Looking for Salvation

Do not trust winter until the very end of it.
Do not trust yourself until your last breath.

1. My son, I shall tell you what my father has told me and what he has heard from his grandfather. Not one of the people that you see around you will still be alive within a hundred years. And of those you do not see, how many of them die each day in hospital wards and prison cells? Besides them, how many humans die during travels or in backbreaking labors or in quarrels and litigations against each other? Of the handful who remain, how many are happy? And are they able to retain their happiness? If not, is it happiness at all?

2. A squirrel is running around in a cage. How great is its desire to reach a pine grove! A worm is gnawing on an apple. Its only concern is whether its sweet world is endless. A mosquito is buzzing in your ear. How full of agitation and passion is that buzz!

Would that the squirrel not run as fast in its cage,
Would that the worm not hasten with finishing its apple,
Would that the mosquito makes somewhat less noise!

Can this advice be helpful to them?
Will they be able to grasp what they should do?
And what about the human?
Will he be able to find himself in his earthly pursuits?

3. The Truth is revealed to all, the honest and the dishonest; but, It will never expose Itself to dishonest hands. The earthly sun shines upon the righteous and the unrighteous but the spiritual Sun will never be radiant in the unrighteous heart.

Mysterious Discourses

4. To build barricades against blizzards, to combat the frost with bonfires on the streets, to break the ice covering the rivers - will all that force the times of cold to depart?

Only spring will bring cold to an end. And those who fought winter in such a way keep saying, "We did a great job!"

5. A villager looks grim for the whole day. The neighbors are in a panic. They start guessing. Maybe their neighbor is planning mischief? Maybe he has it in his mind to lay his hands on a disputed plot of land? Maybe he has even decided to sue someone? So the concerned neighbors go and warn their relatives and their friends. One of them even runs to notify the mayor of the village. Everyone is worried and prepares for the worst. In a few days, they find out what was wrong with their neighbor. His wife had discovered the hiding place that he used to stash away some money! Had his neighbors not given way to their fantasies, they would not have become the laughing stock of the entire countryside.

6. Children desire to endlessly play,
Young people desire to endlessly love,
Middle age people desire to endlessly work,
Old age people desire to endlessly start from the beginning.

7. The shadow of a tree becomes longer in the morning, becomes shorter at noon, again grows longer in the afternoon and finally disappears at dusk. The shadow is in motion, while the tree is not. But, in spite of that, it is the tree that is living, not the shadow.

Ideas come and go, in turn. They are constantly in motion while man's essence does not change. In spite of that, it is man who is living, not his ideas.

8. The ground is being ploughed and furrowed, seed is being sown into it. The ground does not resist. If it were to resist, where would the harvest come from?
Wheat is being milled, flour is being kneaded into dough and dough is being placed into a hot oven.
If wheat were to grumble and refuse processing, where would bread come from?

LOOKING FOR SALVATION

9. In the summer, villagers place scarecrows in their fields and kitchen gardens. Every scarecrow looks different because they all wear the clothes of their respective owners. When it gets windy, the scarecrows start to flap their sleeves, to turn, to bow and even to creak just like their masters. For the birds, they are real human beings.

10. The town authorities set up a lamppost on the street, right by the sidewalk. Some people were happy that the street was now illuminated and that pedestrians would no longer stumble in the darkness. Others were upset saying, "If the lantern goes out of service, one is sure to run into the lamppost and break one's head." Thus an ordinary lamppost can bring joy to some and grief to others.

11. A man ardently dreamed of finding a treasure and getting rich. As time went by, he began to think that the treasure could lie in his own basement, why not? The man grew so sure of it that he began earnestly searching for the treasure and kept doing it until the basement was dug through and through. After that, the man started grieving. When others advised him to forget about the non-existent treasure, he would reply, "But where did I get the idea that the treasure was here? If it were not here, I would have never started searching. I still feel that it is somewhere near." No one was able to dissuade the man before the end of his life.

12. Children draw outlines of different animals in the sand by the sea. They name them "cat", "dog", "horse", "tiger" and happily play with them. And when someone is clumsy enough to step on their drawings, the children break into tears. They are sorry for the animals drawn in the sand. But then, when the children are tired of the game, they just leave everything and run home. And their creatures, cats, dogs, horses and tigers are washed away by the waves.

13. Once upon a time a mighty king ordered that his courtiers compete in lying. The one who managed to produce the greatest lie would be lavishly rewarded. The courtiers strained themselves to invent various stories but not one of their lies impressed the king. Every time he would say, "No. This does not sound like a lie. Something like this can easily happen in reality."

Unexpectedly, there appeared a soldier who stated that he knew the greatest lie. The soldier was brought before the king. He was told that for his insolence, he would be punished by beheading if he was not able to please the king. "Very well," the soldier responded firmly. "I am ready." "Then begin," ordered the king. "The king has died!" the soldier exclaimed loudly. "The king is dead!" "Stop, stop! This is impossible!" the king shouted, confused. "Fine, I agree. This is the greatest lie in the world!"

14. A recently born foal was afraid of everything. He was trembling. He was so weak that he would constantly fall on his knees. When the foal saw big horses that were running, swift and free, across a green meadow, he was so scared that he hid under his mother's belly and from there his thin voice sounded, "Would I really ever become like them?" "Don't be afraid, my child," the mare replied. "You are born to run. There is time for everything. A day will come when you will see how you can dash across the meadow, swift and free."

15. In a kingdom, there was a town where all residents were obliged to wear masks. They became so accustomed to it that they could not recognize each other with their masks off. But there came a time when the old king died and the new king annulled the decrees of the previous reign. So the townsmen had to make acquaintance with one another all over again. And if they were unable to recognize a friend or a relative without a mask, they would try to recall what mask he had been wearing in the past. And they would become amazed at seeing how great the difference was between the mask and the real face.

16. A village prankster came to the riverbank and hung a pitcher on a branch of a tall alder. His fellow villagers, who used to go there to fish, soon noticed the reflection of the pitcher in the water. A rumor began to spread that there was a pitcher filled with gold on the bottom of the river. Many people dove into the river and tried to grasp the pitcher; but alas, they could not find it under water although they were able to see it clearly from the bank! Once a passer-by observed their vain efforts and asked, "What are you looking for?" The villagers explained that they were trying to find a pitcher filled with gold. The passer-by smiled and said, "The pitcher is hanging above your heads and you are looking for it under water."

17. Once a hunter got lost in the mountains. Trying to make his way out of a deep gorge, he stumbled and fell down headlong but he did not get injured because he fell into a lake. The water of the lake was Living Water but the hunter was not aware of that and he did not know how to swim. Having gulped a good amount of water, he managed to come up to the surface and started screaming, "Help! I am dying! I shall

drown!" But the hunter did not drown because the water supported him and he did not die because it was Living Water. With great pains, he reached the shore and saw an inscription on a cliff, "The water of this lake is Living Water. He who tastes the water will live long but he will never find the road to this place again." The hunter made his way out of the gorge and finally reached his home. Indeed, he lived long but he was never able to tell anyone the location of the lake with Living Water.

18. A family living on a distant farm on the edge of the forest received guests. The visitors spent the day with their hosts, admiring the picturesque surroundings and a beautiful pond near the farm. Towards evening, the guests decided to walk to the neighboring village and promised to come back before darkness fell. The hosts advised their guests, "When you walk back, follow the direction of the pond. When you see the pond, you are home."

However, the guests met some old acquaintances in the village and talked with them for quite a while. They decided to go back to the farm only when it was completely dark and rain had started to fall. The villagers offered to accompany them but the guests refused saying that they remembered the road well and would return safely on their own. Unfortunately, they took a wrong turn and started to follow the road leading directly to the pond. It was pitch black so they ended up falling into the pond. "Wonderful!" said one of the guests, as they were climbing out. "It is exactly the pond that they advised us to look for! Now we know precisely where we are!" And, indeed, they saw a light nearby which was the window of the farmhouse where the hosts met them, relieved and happy.

19. Shepherd dogs that guard sheep in the mountains are very ferocious and have a terrifying appearance. So the passers-by prefer to stay away from them. Once it happened that a man did not notice a flock in the valley. When he saw the sheep, it was too late. A pack of angry dogs, scattering on the run to form a semicircle, was approaching him. It was already impossible to escape; so. the man, not knowing what to do, just sat down on the ground, come what may. But, to the man's great surprise, the dogs, having reached their prey, did not attack. Instead, they sat at a small distance from him and remained there, furious as they were. As soon as the man moved, the dogs were ready to jump on him; so, he preferred to stay motionless. In a short while, the shepherds ran up to the spot and drove the dogs away. They were quite surprised

to see the man safe and sound. "It was smart of you to sit down and not move. Only because of that they did not hurt you," the shepherds told the man.

20. When a candle is reflected in a multitude of mirrors that surround it,
    it is difficult to find the real candle.
When a goldfish is swimming in an aquarium made of mirrored glass,
    it is impossible to distinguish the live fish from its reflection.

21. A group of devoted scientists was very eager to find some previously unknown species. The scientists would roam the mountains looking for unusual footprints and thoroughly questioned the locals. One day, the inhabitants of a small village deep in the wilderness told the researchers that a strange animal had been noticed in the surroundings. The scientists examined the nearby paths and indeed discovered some bizarre footprints. At night, sounds would reach them from the mountain slopes and it appeared that some creature was wandering there.

The rumors about these phenomena soon reached the city. Curious people started to go to the mountains for their summer vacations. To accommodate them, the locals built several inns and hotels and a road was built to the village that was in the center of activity. Articles about the search for the unknown animal were regularly published in popular science magazines in spite of the fact that no one had succeeded in actually finding it. Gradually, the small village in the wilderness turned into a resort town and old men would laugh amongst themselves, "Of course, no one has ever seen such an animal around here. We were so good in forging its footprints and spreading rumors about it that our village became a prosperous resort."

22. A boy and his father liked to fly a kite together. The boy wrote his own name on it and would imagine that it was he, himself, soaring in the sky. As time went by, that idea became embedded in his heart. But once a strong gust of wind broke the cord the kite was bound to; so, the kite fell to the ground and broke. The boy cried and could not be consoled. He kept telling everyone that it was he, himself, who had crashed to death together with the kite. But the boy's father managed to calm him down. "My son, you were always here, by my side," he said. "It was the kite that crashed. You are alive and can make another kite, if you wish. Remember. You are just guiding the kite. You are not flying. So, you cannot crash together with it."

LOOKING FOR SALVATION

23. Two men were traveling in the mountains. They came to an area where unusual rock formations resembled figures of human beings, beasts, and some fantastic creatures. "Look!" exclaimed one of the travelers. "Here is a woman's head!" The other one looked and said, "No. This is an old man's head!" They started to argue. Each was trying to prove that he was right. Then it occurred to them that they should switch places. "Now it's clear!" both men exclaimed. "From one place, you see a woman's head and from the other place, an old man's head!" although in both instances the images were just weathered rocks.

24. A woodcutter knew that wild beasts were dangerous for man. The beasts can instantly become infuriated and attack anything that moves. "If you see a bear, do not run, stay still," experienced people advised him. Those words remained in his memory. Once, in the spring, the woodcutter was walking through the forest. All of a sudden, a she-bear with two cubs appeared on the path just a few meters in front of him. The she-bear turned her huge head in the man's direction and gazed attentively. The woodcutter stopped, stiff with fear. The she-bear sniffed the scent of the man standing still and studied him with suspicion. The cubs ran off into the thicket and the she-bear, not having discovered anything threatening, crossed the path without haste and followed her cubs. "Oh yes, those people were right," the woodcutter said to himself, recovering from his fright. "Their advice came in handy."

25. A man had a good friend in the time of his youth. Whenever he remembered his friend, he always turned up. At times, the man tended to forget about his friend and would not see him for a long time, but would still constantly feel his friend's care and help.

After a while, the man got married and became the father of children. More and more rarely he would recall his friend. Soon, the concerns about the family's well being began to drain all of his energy. He frequently got sick and ended up in the hospital. Neither his wife nor his children were able to help him in any way and his other relatives were preoccupied by their own troubles. When the man felt that he was getting worse, he remembered his long-forgotten friend and the friend came to the hospital right away. He paid all the bills and made sure the man was well taken care of. The patient's state started to improve. Only then did the man start to seriously think about his life. No one was able to do as much for him during the time of his misfortune as his friend. How could he show-appreciation for his friend's kindness and concern? The man decided from that time on, he would always treat his friend with warmth and love and would never forget him. In a short while, his friend came once more to visit him and said, "My dear, only the illness changed your attitude towards me. If you had followed my advice all those years, you would have seen an even greater love towards you and your life would have taken quite a different course."

26. A big sycamore tree was growing on the street spreading its branches wide in front of a house. Passers-by would often praise it saying, "What a great and beautiful tree and how much shade it gives! How pleasant it is to rest under it when it gets hot!" At times, other voices would say, "You know how many leaves this tree sheds in the autumn? Besides, in the winter entire branches fall down and one has to toil taking all that off the street." All those words did not make the sycamore tree bigger or smaller. It always remained the same.

27. In the depth of the garden, there stood a big old stump of a chestnut tree, gnarled and overgrown with moss. A boy liked to play in that garden. More than anything in the world, he was afraid of the terrible tree-stump because the boy was taking it for a wicked bandit from a fairy tale. "Bandit, bandit!" the boy would scream, running back to his parents in the house. One evening, the boy's father took him by the hand and walked with him right to the horrible tree-stump. "Look carefully and do not fear. You don't see any bandit do you?" "Now I don't," the boy responded. "But when I am afraid of him, the bandit appears and when I am not afraid, he disappears."

28. Once in the summer, a young man was walking through the woods. He was not able to reach home before dark and had to spend the night in the forest. It started to drizzle. The young man settled under a pine tree and made a campfire. At first, while the fire was burning, the young man felt confident. But when he prepared to go to sleep, the fire had already died out and the youth started feeling uneasy. Now he would hear a branch crackling somewhere, now the wind would swing the tops of the pine trees, now some unknown sounds would emerge from the very depth of the thicket. It appeared to the young man that the forest was full of various beasts and terrible monsters. He started to recall different horror stories about forest encounters and it gave him the shivers. But then the young man thought, "I am completely alone in this forest and there is no one around me" and his fear disappeared at once. He continued to think, "All of these forest sounds are quite natural. Had there been

LOOKING FOR SALVATION

beasts nearby, the smoke from the campfire would have scared them away. Therefore, those were just my own fears and if some problems do occur, I shall think how to solve them then, not now." In this way, the young man calmed down completely and fell asleep. Whenever he woke up in the darkness, he would recall that he had no one and nothing to be afraid of because all fears existed only in him and he would fall asleep again. From that time on, the young man was never afraid to spend a night in the woods alone.

29. To aim to climb the summit and to reach only the mountain pass,
    is better than not to start at all.
To desire to move to the capital city and to settle in its suburb,
    is better than to stay home in the village.
To visit an interesting country even in transit,
    is better than just to hear stories about it.
To comprehend even part of the Truth,
    is better than not to know It at all.

30. The forester sees forest, while the woodcutter sees trees.
The captain sees ocean, while the fisherman sees fish.
The passer-by sees fields, while the peasant sees land.
The pilgrim sees sky, while the seaman sees clouds.

31. As long as the house is vacant, there are no concerns about repairs.
As long as the field is not sown, there are no concerns about the harvest.
As long as there are no fish in the pond, there are no fishermen in sight.
As long as there are no bad thoughts in the heart, there is no trouble.

32. When a man is just learning to swim, it is completely incomprehensible to him how it is done. But as soon as he starts to swim, everything becomes clear.
When a man first hears about the Truth, it is completely incomprehensible to him what it is all about. But as soon as he learns the Truth, everything becomes clear.

33. A city dweller came to the countryside and went to the forest to pick berries together with a villager. They got somewhat carried away by the picking and after a while found themselves in a marshy area. The villager noticed danger and warned the city dweller, "Now we must be cautious. We must stick to the path by which we came

because towards the right there is a swamp and towards the left, a quagmire." "And what is the difference between them?" the city man asked. "Really not much, only in the quagmire you go down faster."

34. Once there was a prince who heard about a beautiful young princess living in a far-away land. He decided to win her heart and departed with a small retinue. After some days of travel, he and his companions were met by a great army of the princess. The commanding general told the prince that in order to see the princess, he would first have to cross swords with him. In the course of the fierce fight, the prince cast his adversary on the ground and the general begged for mercy. He said that he was ready to surrender with his entire army if only the prince would go back to his native land. But the prince refused the offer saying that he desired to see the princess. He released the general and his troops allowed the prince and his retinue to pass.

Soon the castle of the princess appeared. Ministers and servants came out to meet the prince with opulent gifts. They offered him various treasures should he agree to turn back. But the prince insisted that they let him see the princess. When the prince and princess finally met, they fell in love. The princess consented to go with the prince to his country. When they departed, they were followed by the entire army, led by the general, all ministers and servants with the treasures of the princess.

35. A young man learned that somewhere in the world there was a stone that could fulfill wishes. He desired to find that stone and started to ask various people, trying to encounter someone who could help him. But in his land, no one knew anything about the stone. So the young man set forth as a wanderer. He went from one country to another until he was told that in one distant land there lived a wise man who knew where the stone could be found. After a long and difficult journey, the tired youth finally faced the wise man. "Are you not a native of such-and-such country," the wise man asked? "Yes", replied the youth. "I came to you from that country." "And are you not a resident of such-and-such city, living in a house by a lake?" "Yes, I truly live there," replied the perplexed youth. "Well", the wise man declared, "It is known to me that the miraculous stone is set in the wall of your room, in that very house where you live." "So I must return home after such an exhausting journey?!" "If you had not reached me, overcoming so many obstacles," replied the wise man, "how would you have learned where you could find the miraculous stone?"

LOOKING FOR SALVATION

36. Only he who sees nothing will be able to find the secret chamber with no walls, no ceiling and no floor.
Only he who knows nothing will be able to settle there.
Only he who does not know how to talk will be able to tell about it.
Only he who is completely deaf will be able to hear what they tell him.
And only he who has nothing will be able to possess what is located in the secret chamber.

37. In the land of the blind, a one-eyed man is king.
In the land of kings, an ordinary man is a rarity.
In the land of fools, a reasonable man is a great scholar.
In the land of great scholars, a simple-hearted man is a rare treasure.

38. For whales, the ocean is a cradle.
For an ant, a puddle is a stormy sea.
For swallows, the sky is their native home.
For mosquitoes, a slight breeze is a source of worry.

39. The eagle does not get tired of flying.
The cow does not get bored of chewing its cud.
The dog does not break its teeth gnawing on bones.
Man's heart can never be filled too much with God.

40. To end up in a pot, it is enough for a fish to swallow the bait but once.
To become a thief, it is enough to steal but once.
To fall into an abyss, it is enough to step but once.
To experience innumerable woes, one bad thought is enough

41. One can recognize his father and his mother in any crowd.
If food is tasty, there is no doubt about it.
One can distinguish the aroma of a fragrant rose from all other scents.
The song of the nightingale in the forest cannot be confused with the voices of other birds.

42. Wherever the fox runs, it always returns to its burrow.
Swifts in the spring return to their old nests.

Mysterious Discourses

Every bee knows its hive.
Wherever man's desires roam, they always return to the heart.

43. A thief in an unknown house is frightened by his own shadow.
A hare in the woods is scared even by a falling leaf.
A wild beast is afraid of daylight.
A lonely man is afraid of himself.

44. Look for lost spectacles on your own forehead.
The lost bucket will be found in the well.
The fish that disappeared from the table will be seen in the cat's claws.
If you are looking for the Truth, look for It in your heart.

45. When a mother takes the crying baby in her arms, he calms down right away.
When the fragrance of a rose reaches one's nostrils, there is no need to say that it has bloomed.
When a child has fallen asleep, there is no need to explain to him that he sleeps.
When man finds God, he understands It himself.

46. If you keep pushing the carpenter's arm, the job will be ruined.
If you keep lecturing the driver while he is at the wheel, an accident will be imminent.
If you keep showing the smith where he must strike, you can lose your finger.
If you keep talking and never listen, you will find no one to converse with.

47. When a dog is chasing a hare, it will not be led astray.
When a cat is playing with a captive mouse, you cannot lure it with a fish.
When a bear finds honey, it loses all fear.
When a rich man sees money, he forgets about everything in the world.

48. If you do not want to lose anything, own nothing.
If you do not want to roam, do not leave your house.
If you dislike noise, do not visit a marketplace.
If you are looking for peace, do not have any cares.

49. A man's wife died. Struck by grief, he neglected all his affairs and fell into a deep melancholy. The rooms of his house became full of litter and dust. And the man,

himself, appeared completely wasted. His neighbor felt pity for the poor widower and advised him to at least go and wash his face. "What for?" the widower replied. "One of my rooms is all litter, the other one is all dust. I shall never be able to wash myself clean." "If you, in your house, have litter in one room and dust in the other, then either clean them up or don't enter there at all!" the neighbor exclaimed. "Just rub your eyes clean and you will see at once what to do."

50. A man was very fond of birds. In his house, he had numerous cages where he kept his birds to whom he was much attached. He fed them, gave them water, cleaned the cages and admired the birds' singing. But, as time went by, the man started to feel overburdened by all the tasks he had to fulfill to take care of his birds. He told a friend about his anguish. "Let them go," the friend advised, "And you will be free of all the cares." "I could let them go," the bird fancier said. "The problem is that they are not letting me go."

51. So many birds chirp joyfully in the forest and there are hardly any hungry ones among them.
Many beasts are roaming in the woods and you never see any that are just skin and bone.
An infant is feeding only on his mother's milk and is not preoccupied with what he is going to eat in the evening.
The world follows the one who follows the Truth.

52. Once a geologist was walking across the desert back to his camp. He was trapped by a sand storm, lost his way and started to roam the desert. He took care to save his supply of water but after a while he drank the last drop and the geologist felt he was weakening. He climbed a sand dune and saw a tiny oasis: a small water source, some grass and a few bushes. The geologist spent several days there, feeding on his last loaf of bread. He was afraid to go away from the water because he was not sure he had sufficient strength to reach the camp or, should he fail, to return to the spring. The geologist reflected and made a final decision, "It is better to die near a spring than to roam the sands." He was ready to abide by this decision to the end. And when the man was starting to lose hope, the drovers of a caravan that was passing by noticed him and he was saved.

53. Solitude in a city is harder than in a desert.
Estrangement of a loved one is more painful than life among unfamiliar people.
The silent reproach of your kin hurts more than open reprimands.
Friendly support is better than solemn vows and promises.

54. Look for the exit where you have entered.
Descend where you have ascended.
Finish where you have started.
Continue where you have stopped.

55. What you are striving for is in constant retreat.
What you are trying to go away from is in constant pursuit.
Leave everything to the people and they will leave you.
Let everything be what it is.

56. A long time ago, a villager noticed a cave high up in the mountains, in an almost inaccessible cliff. He recalled a legend that somewhere in this area, the treasures of the ancient kings were hidden. With extreme difficulty, he reached the cave. The man entered and saw a copper door near the cave's mouth. He opened the door and came into a chamber with heaps of copper coins lying on the ground. Without delay, the mountaineer filled all his pockets with coins, stuffed as many as he could under his shirt and prepared to return home.

After closing the copper door behind him, he noticed another door, somewhat deeper inside the cave. That door was made of silver. The man opened it and saw a chamber full of silver coins. He quickly threw out the copper money and stuffed silver wherever he could.

He was again ready to leave, but at that moment he discovered in the darkness yet another door, this time made of gold. The mountaineer threw the door open. The chamber behind it was full of gold coins. Hastily, he threw out the silver and loaded himself up with gold so that he was hardly able to move. Finally, he could leave for sure.

But right by the cave's opening, the mountaineer saw a wooden door, dusty and obviously very old. Hesitatingly, he opened it. There was nothing inside the chamber except for a simple wooden staff placed on a stone. The mountaineer took the staff, bewildered. Not knowing what to do with it, he struck the staff against the floor. At once, extraordinary precious ornaments and gems started to pour from somewhere. The man was numb with fascination, the staff slipped away from his hands and the flow of jewels stopped. The man realized that with the staff in his possession, he would need none of the treasures of the cave. He threw away all the gold, took only the staff and left the cave forever.

57. A resident of a distant province was very interested in the capital of his country. He yearned to know what it looked like. What landmarks, monuments, squares and parks the city had. But there was no one he could ask. Living far away from the center of the country, he was not familiar with anyone who had visited the capital. So he had to content himself with collecting photographs, postcards and newspaper articles about the city he loved. Once, due to a lucky chance, he finally had an opportunity to go to the capital himself. When he had walked the city through and through and felt more confident in it, he was handed a letter from his fellow-townsmen. They were informing him that they had found an old man who, in the time of his youth, had briefly seen the capital and still remembered a few things about the city. "Friends, but what need do I have now in listening to someone's stories about the capital," the man wrote back? "I am already here myself."

58. A man's wife left him and he was terribly upset, to the extent that he fell into despair, became ill and was taken to a psychiatric hospital. After regaining his senses, he asked the doctors to let him return home but was told that the course of treatment was not yet over. The man was indignant and started to argue. They gave him an injection by force, so the patient fell asleep. After he woke up, the man felt a terrible headache and cramps in his entire body. He was afraid for his life; so, he decided not to allow the personnel to give him any more injections. The man informed the doctors about it, after which he was again forcefully injected with an even more powerful dose. Having regained consciousness, the man realized that resistance was fruitless. He decided to stop arguing with the doctors, to be calm and patient and not to complain. Very soon, he noticed that the personnel started to treat him differently. There were no more injections and, after a while, he was no longer given pills as well. Finally, there came a day when he was discharged from the hospital.

59. The great ocean does not make any effort to be great.
Big rivers are the quietest ones, but they flow far.

Mysterious Discourses

High mountains do not grow high at someone else's expense.
Humble people are not in the spotlight but they are more reliable than many others.

60. Once a merchant came to a far-away country and entered a strange city where all the residents wore shackles. The merchant thought, "And if they shackle me as well, what should I do then?" That very moment, the guards approached and, having noticed a new free man, immediately put him in irons. The merchant realized he could no longer return home and started losing heart. He tried to question the unfortunate residents of the city why all of them were shackled. They replied that such was an age-old custom of the city. "So all people of this city are doomed to wear shackles until they die?" the merchant asked. The people responded, "It is rumored that sometimes there comes to the city an old man who is free and does not wear shackles. Only that man knows how one can become free. But he appears so rarely that many of us are in doubt whether it is true." "There is nothing I can do but wait," the merchant thought. "Perhaps I shall be able to meet that old man and learn how to free myself."

Many years passed. The merchant grew older and his hair started to turn gray but one day he suddenly saw an old man walking freely by on the street unshackled. "Grandpa," the captive exclaimed, "Help me to get rid of my irons!" "My son," replied the old man, "All you have to do is to say inwardly, 'Let the guards unshackle me at once.' Then you will be free." The captive thought that it was just a harsh joke but still he decided to try and pronounced inwardly the magic phrase. Immediately, the guards appeared and unshackled him. The astonished merchant hurried to leave the strange city. Outside the city gates, he saw the old man again. "Grandpa, please tell me, what is the secret of this city," he begged him? "This city is not easy to understand," replied the old man. "Here one becomes a captive and goes free by the medium of his thoughts. You were saved only because you believed my words. And those who do not believe me remain captives of the city and there is nothing else I can do for them."

61. Friendship with a lion can end badly.
Where wolves abound, it is better not to pasture sheep.
You cannot chase dogs away with a bone.
You will not get rid of bad thoughts if you obey them.

LOOKING FOR SALVATION

62. Due to the slander of some malevolent people, a man ended up in a horrible prison from which no one emerged alive. The prison had been built by a sorcerer and his servants were guarding the unfortunate prisoners. The new inmate tried to escape through various means but every time he failed. The infuriated guards beat him heavily and finally transferred him to a solitary cell on death row. Here the prisoner discovered a tiny crack in the wall in which there was a yellowed piece of paper with the following words, "There is only one way to escape from this prison. All other methods are fruitless. Once every ten years at night, the sorcerer's forces weaken and the cell door remains unlocked. That night you may be able to escape. Remember as you go, you must keep silent regardless of what you see. The corridor makes three turns and each turn is manned by a guard who possesses magic powers. The guards will create terrible images in order to stop you. If you say a single word, you are lost."

When the long-awaited night finally came, the prisoner discovered that the door of his cell really was unlocked. He came out and started walking slowly. At the first turn, before he even reached the guard box, he suddenly saw his old mother, moribund, asking him to stop and bid her farewell. The poor inmate, recalling what the note said, with a tremendous effort forced himself to keep on going. At the next turn, right by the guard box, the man saw his father, who was agonizing and begging him to approach and say but a few words. The prisoner, torn by pity, still kept silent and walked on faster. Behind the third guard box, there was an exit from the terrible prison. Right outside, the inmate saw his wife and son, who were running towards him, overjoyed. And at that very moment, a huge torrent of water roared, flooding the street. People were screaming that the dam had collapsed, and the city was being flooded. The prisoner rushed to save his wife and son but they were caught in a whirlpool and went under. "My wife! My son!" the poor man screamed in horror, unable to withstand the sight. At that very moment, he found himself back in his cell.

63. It is easy to understand lies but it is difficult to understand Truth,
That is why there are a lot of lies in the world and Truth is rare.
People are quick to believe in lies and cannot accept Truth,
Because lying is comfortable and Truth is not.

64. A thief appears and your pocket is empty.
A tiny hole in a barrel and the wine is gone.

Mysterious Discourses

A small mouse in a jar and the oil is spoiled.
A little bad thought and all joy leaves the heart.

65. A flock of birds was flying to Africa for the winter. Young birds that were going to see Africa for the first time were agitated, uneasy, made noise and asked numerous questions: "Is it really hot in Africa? Are there rivers in Africa? Are there forests? Does it rain in Africa?" The leader of the flock at first answered all the questions but grew tired and said, "You know what, children? The main thing is to reach Africa and there you will have nothing to worry about."

66. A man went fishing with some old friends and took his teenage son with him. The adults, seeing that the boy did not know how to do anything, began to teach him how to make a campfire, how to secure a pot over it, how to clean fish and how to wash dishes. The boy would often argue and get upset, feeling that he was clumsy. He approached his father and said, "Dad, I learned many new things but I can't do them all well. That hurts me and I get tired because of it." "Son," the father replied, "Just be humble all the time and you will feel better." A few days passed, the boy came up to his father again, "Dad, I keep being humble and I get tired of it even more. Is it okay if I take a rest from humility for a day?"

67. Young soldiers were in combat for the first time. They were very afraid to die; so, they were constantly ducking, taking shelter from bullets and shells and almost panicked. There were many wounded among them. When the battle was over, the young soldiers asked a weathered veteran to teach them how to survive. "Is the key to dig trenches deeper, to always hug the ground and move on all fours? "All of that is good," the veteran soldier said. "But the best is to learn to sacrifice yourself for the sake of others. Only in this way can you survive. Death is afraid of good people."

68. On weekends, when the husband and the wife stayed home together, they would frequently argue, get annoyed and tell each other many offensive things. Steaming with anger, the husband would go outside in order to regain himself. By the entrance, there was a bench and an old woman used to rest there while her tiny dog would run nearby. Once the man noticed that sometimes the dog barked at him angrily, while at other times, when he returned home from work, it did not pay any attention to him. He decided to ask the old woman why her dog was acting in such a way. "Oh

LOOKING FOR SALVATION

dear," she replied. "My little one always senses whenever people are angry or irritated and barks at them. And when people are calm, the dog does not even notice them."

69. A sick man's thoughts are about his illness.
A healthy man's are about his marriage.
Thoughts about sensual delights come to the hedonist.
Thoughts about salvation come to the man who is seeking God.

70. Because the wind blows, flour is ground at the mill.
Because the ball is round, everyone likes it.
Because the man is soft, he can be a good friend.
Because the man is faithful, he can be trusted.

71. A decrepit wall, one day will collapse.
A tall pine, one day will fall.
A snake that entered the house, one day will bite.
A bad thought, if you are not careful, will surely lead to death.

72. Streams in the waterfall incessantly fall down,
But the waterfall itself does not fall.
The sea waves constantly run ashore,
But the sea itself does not move anywhere.
Know the depth of the heart and you will be steadfast.

73. A cuckoo in the woods hears only the echo of its own voice.
Winter frost creates a different pattern on every windowpane.
In every drop of dew there is a sun.
In every human heart there is a universe.

74. Where forest paths diverge, it is not easy to understand where to go.
If there is fog over the sea, it is hard to determine where the coast is.
Blue sky is everywhere high.
In the middle of the ocean, all shores are distant.

75. The one who vacillates knows nothing yet.
The one who knows does not vacillate.

He who doubts will find himself back where he started.
He who is firm in his faith will emerge from all troubles unhurt.

76. There are many seeds in a sunflower on a single stalk.
A flock of birds spends the night on a single tree.
Seagulls from the entire coast nest on a single island.
Bad thoughts come to the one who consents to them.

77. A peasant living on a distant farm sheltered a bandit out of pity. After some time, the bandit left and returned with his companions in crime. The peasant was weak-willed so he allowed them to stay and soon his house turned into a den. The bandits were bringing all their loot there. When the gang was caught, the peasant went to trial along with the bandits as their accomplice. "So how did you become a bandit?" the judge asked him severely. The peasant sighed heavily, "Due to a lack of character, Your Honor!"

78. A five year-old boy was afraid to stay home alone when his parents left to attend to their business. As soon as they stepped outside, everything in the house seemed to come alive. The boy was frightened by the striking of the clock, by the howling of wind in the attic and by the rustle of branches against the windowpane. It always seemed to him that someone was walking in the house while it was only the quiet ticking of the table clock. When his parents returned home, the boy would always tell them how scared he had been without them. "Don't be afraid, son," his father used to tell him. "In the house, there is nothing at all to be afraid of." "I know, Dad," the boy would reply. "And still it is scary."

79. Rare animals hide in the most impenetrable thickets.
Rare metals lie deep in the earth.
Modesty is far from high rank and fame.
The most unremarkable man is the support for all.

80. The nearer rain is, the lower swallows fly.
The less a patient is irritable, the better he is looked after.
The lower a lake is, the more rivers fall into it.
The lower the head is, the closer the heart is to God.

LOOKING FOR SALVATION

81. When you are carrying medicine to a gravely ill man, don't be delayed anywhere.
When you are trying to catch up with someone, better mind your feet.
When you are treating someone to a meal, don't count your expenses.
When you are lending money, don't expect it to be returned.

82. A fox prefers to gnaw off its own paw to escape from the trap.
A fish jumps out of the water when being pursued.
A drowning man is not worried that his hat has sunk.
To guard the heart against a bad thought is more important than to save yourself from death.

83. Regardless of how big a wheel is, it always touches the ground at its lowest part.
A stone falls lower whenever possible.
The most necessary part of a shoe is the sole.
The best man is the humble one.

84. The rainbow is beautiful because it does not admire itself.
The flowers that give a sweet fragrance are most loved.
A cloud that does not bring rain is worthy of regret.
Attachments are a ditch that is hard to jump over.

85. A herald was sent to the king to inform him about the defeat of his army. The herald knew that whoever brought such a message would be beheaded. While on the way, he thought of a ruse that could save his life. When the herald was brought into the throne hall, he fell to his knees begging the king to pardon him because he had completely forgotten the message. The king and his ministers reflected, "On the one hand, the herald was clearly worthy of death for such a breach of duty, but, on the other hand, should his life be spared so there remained hope that he would remember the important message." So for the time being they decided not to execute him. Soon the tragic news reached the king through a different channel and the herald was saved.

86. For a ropewalker, the rope is the only way.
A blind man cannot leave home without his cane.
He whose leg is in a cast should not lose his crutches.
In the spiritual life without a pure heart, you cannot make a single step.

Mysterious Discourses

87. A young geologist set out on an expedition into the mountains. At first, he had trouble breathing and working and he suffered from insomnia. His colleagues tried to reassure him, "You will get used to the high altitude and feel better." After some time, the geologist started to get accustomed to the mountain air. He was efficient in his work and even traveled by foot. When they told him to briefly return to the city to take care of some business, he was reluctant to leave the mountains that he had already gotten used to and had even come to love.

In the city they asked the geologist, "Well, young man, did you find anything in the mountains?" "Yes," he replied. "I found patience."

88. Once a minister was falsely accused of a very serious crime: a plot against the king. The minister was not guilty and at every interrogation denied his participation in the plot. The king decided to test the minister. The following royal decree was to be read to the prisoner, "If the accused persists in the denial of guilt, he shall be executed as an obstinate and unrepentant criminal. If the accused admits to his participation in the plot, he shall be sentenced to life imprisonment." However, the guards and the executioner had been instructed to execute the prisoner if he admitted his guilt. And if he continued to insist on his innocence, he was to be left alive and sent into exile.

After the executioner finished reading the royal decree to the prisoner, he said gravely, "Say your last word. If you admit your guilt, say "yes", and you shall save your life. And if you say "no", you shall be executed as an obstinate and unrepentant evildoer." The minister firmly answered, "No!" The execution was not carried out.

89. A sleeping man dreamed that he was looking in the mirror and not seeing his reflection in it. When he woke up, he remembered the dream, was terrified, and rushed to the mirror. But the reflection was there, as usual, so the man smiled with relief and said, "As long as we are two, I am alive." A servant, who heard these words remarked, "Master, without the mirror you are not sure you are alive, are you?"

90. Only a single thread fits into a needle's eye.
One climbs up by a single ladder.
A doctor receives patients only one by one.
The highest summit is only one.

LOOKING FOR SALVATION

91. City dwellers are like stars in the sky. It appears that they are close to each other, but in reality great distances lie between them.
In a dense crowd, people are hugging each other, but it does not make them happy.
Birds of a flock stay together, but in case of danger they are quick to disperse.
Every encounter except the encounter with Truth is the beginning of separation.

92. Things that make one look back:
a blooming lilac,
a rainbow over a field,
snow-covered summits at sunset,
pure and beautiful eyes of a maiden,
kind and wise countenance of an old man.

93. When a turtledove is hatching its eggs, the entire world disappears for it.
When a nightingale sings, it hears nothing except its own song.
When a cat sees a mouse, nothing else matters to it.
When a tailor is threading a needle, he sees only the needle's eye.

94. He who is drowning needs a life belt, not instructions on how to swim.
He who is asking to borrow some money needs help,
   not a conversation about friendship.
He who is freezing at night needs a blanket,
   not the address of a store where they are sold.
He who is looking for spiritual support will not be consoled by books about kindness.

95. Two peasants worked in a field until noon. It was very hot and one of them suggested to the other to go down to the river for a swim. On the way, they were talking about how nice it was to have a river nearby. They reached the bank, took off their clothes and dove into the river. When the two of them came to the surface, one of the peasants said, "By the way, we have not finished the talk about our river." "But what is the use of it now" his friend replied? "Instead of talking about the river, let us swim in it instead!"

96. Duckweed does not withstand running water.
Bats never fly in the sunlight.

Mysterious Discourses

Pigs do not bathe in mountain streams.
Bad thoughts do not live in a good heart.

97. A blind man came to a police precinct to get an ID. He was received by an officer who was a big, heavy man with a high, shrieking voice. Another blind man had an appointment with a doctor who possessed a hoarse and loud voice although he was short and frail. Afterwards the two blind men met and started to talk. "How is it possible that our police force hires such dwarfs," the first blind man asked? "I always thought that police officers were tall and strong." "And I had a doctor's appointment today," the other blind man said. "Such a huge fellow with a hoarse voice! I wonder how he can even be a doctor."

98. Butterflies dash towards fire and they perish.
Iron shavings move towards a magnet and they get stuck to it.
A fish swallows bait and it ends up in the pot.
People endlessly multiply their desires and they run out of time to fulfill them.

99. To shake dynamite in your hands,
To taste hydrochloric acid,
To let a snake bite you,
Is the same as to consent to a bad thought.

100. Wherever you go, you will be followed by:
The blessings of your father,
The grateful memory of those whom you helped,
The prayers of your elders.

And wherever you go, you will always be pursued by:
The memory of your bad deeds,
The hostility of those whom you offended,
The hatred towards yourself and those who stood in your way.

Chapter Two
Getting a Prayer

It is dangerous to cling:
To a woman's love,
To people's praise,
To a traitor's hand,
To a rotten rope,
To this world.

1. A young married couple is going to the sea for their vacation. "I can imagine how we are riding in a train," the wife says, daydreaming. "I can imagine how we are sunbathing on the beach," the husband replies playfully. So they say good-bye to their parents and leave for the railway station. On the way, their car suddenly breaks down; so, they are late for the train and have to call the parents and tell them they are returning home. "We can imagine the faces they have now," the parents sigh.

2. A scientist and a worker were trapped by a snowstorm in the Arctic. They were lost and exhausted. The worker saw a protected slope and offered to dig a shelter in the snow so that they could take refuge there until the storm was over. They began to dig in the frozen snow with their hands. "I have learned so much," the scientist groaned. "And now all that knowledge is of no use to me at all!" "You better forget all you have learned for now and dig faster if you want to live!" the worker said.

3. The king and his retinue were passing through a village. The king found the place pleasant to look at and he desired to converse with members of the community. A delegation was quickly formed. The little son of one of the delegates was begging his father to take him to see the king. The boy was crying so his father finally agreed. When the king appeared, the peasants bent their knees and the king began to address them. The little boy touched his father's shoulder from behind and whispered, "Dad, and what is this fabric that the king's cloak is made of? And what is this hat he is

wearing?" The father looked over cautiously and whispered back, "Son, just look. Don't say a word. Otherwise you will see only the hat but not the czar himself."

4. Once a good maiden fell ill and the doctors were at a loss how to cure her. Her two brothers promised their parents that they would save their sister. In the mountainous part of their kingdom, there lived a wizard. The brothers hurried to him and asked for advice. "In the distant mountains there is an orchard with magic apples that can cure any illness," the old man said. "But terrible monsters roam around the orchard. Those monsters are capable of reading one's mind. If a man is afraid of them, the monsters will tear him apart right away. Only he who is courageous will be able to enter the orchard and gather the magic fruit." "Yes, that is dangerous," the brothers agreed. "But we shall give our lives for the sake of our sister." "Then forward!" the wizard exclaimed. "I shall give you yet another piece of advice. If you follow it, you shall not perish. As soon as you see the monsters, start to inwardly repeat the magic word, 'Hanestra'! Do it unceasingly."

The brothers departed, and after a long journey they finally saw the magic orchard. At that very moment, horrible monsters emerged from the thicket and rushed towards them. "Hanestra! Hanestra! Hanestra!" the brothers repeated and went forward bravely. The monsters stood still, perplexed. The young men entered the orchard, gathered the magic apples and walked back out past the immobile monsters, repeating the miraculous words. Soon they were by their sister's bedside. She tasted the magic fruit and became even more beautiful than before.

5. A scientist traveled to a country where people's speech resembled the murmur of a spring. After returning home, he told his family about his journey and about the language of that country, similar to the sounds produced by running water. Once, the man and his little son were walking through a forest. They sat down to rest at a clearing on the edge of which a small spring was running. The boy listened attentively and said, "Dad, do you hear? Someone here can also speak that language!"

6. Two teenage brothers wanted to treat themselves and their friend to some strawberries. They did not ask their parents' permission and just sneaked into the garden. Their friend, savoring the free desert, repeated all the time, "Great strawberries! Fantastic! The best I have ever eaten!" The brothers whispered to him, "You better eat the strawberries, not chatter about them. The parents may hear you."

GETTING A PRAYER

7. A family lived on the first floor above the shop of a bird salesman. Once their little boy was standing on the balcony and heard loud voices. Someone below was shouting, "Give me your money! Give me your money! I'll shoot! I'll shoot! Police! Police!" The boy was frightened and ran to his father's study. "Dad, Dad!" the boy screamed. "Some people below want money. They are ready to shoot! And someone is calling the police!" "No, son," the father laughed. "They have just brought a parrot to the shop."

8. An old watchman guarded a cherry orchard. At dawn, a bird of rare beauty used to fly into the orchard and peck at the cherries. The old man admired the bird's extraordinary appearance and did not chase it away. He told his grandchildren about the bird and they begged their granddad to let them see it. Early in the morning, the watchman woke the children up and said, "Come out to the orchard quietly. It is here!" The children ran out and rushed towards the gates of the orchard, bumping against each other and making noise. "I'll be the first to look at it! No, me! No, me!" the children were shouting. After discovering nothing in the orchard, they asked, "Granddad, where is the beautiful bird?" "Oh, you little rascals!" he replied. "That bird does not like noise and shouting that is why it flew away!"

9. In the mountains, a young man discovered a cave with very beautiful, but fragile stalactites. "This is a true wonder!" he exclaimed, overjoyed. Suddenly the stones forming the cave's walls started to move and some even fell down. By some miracle, the cave did not collapse. The young man left the cave cautiously but told a friend about his discovery. The friend also wanted to see the cave. "Just stay silent," the young man warned him! When the friend saw the stalactites, he could not suppress a shout, "Oh, my!" At that very moment, stones started to fall down sounding like thunder. A cloud of dust rose and the two friends were lucky to jump out of the cave the beauty of which was disappearing in front of their eyes.

10. During a storm, you don't see a single boat at sea,
During dead calm, you don't see a single wave.
Man's heart may become like heaven,
Or may turn into a storehouse of bad thoughts.

Mysterious Discourses

11. A magician's aides are sawing his assistant in half. The audience applauds. At that moment, the magician's magic closet falls right on him. The audience applauds even louder. "No, no! This is not my trick!" the magician groans.

12. There was a city where the king built a strange edifice and announced to his subjects, "Whoever enters it, may take as much gold as he can carry." The citizens rushed to the edifice but discovered a sign at the entrance, "For the dumb only." So they found a dumb man and sent him inside, expecting him to bring back a bundle of gold. The dumb man entered but came out soon. He asked for a pen and paper and wrote, "There is a second door with a sign, "For the deaf only." The citizens found a man who was deaf and dumb, explained to him what they wanted and sent him inside the building. He also emerged soon and wrote, "There is another door with a sign, "For the blind only." The people took great pains to find a man who was dumb, deaf and blind. They finally found such a man but how could they explain to him what they wanted him to do? At last, it occurred to someone to carve the words of their request on a wooden board. The man who was deaf, dumb and blind understood what he had to do, went and returned with gold.

13. If you don't throw stones in the lake, there will be no circles on the water.
If you don't push boulders off the cliff, no dust will arise.
If you don't walk around the hive, the bees won't bite you.
If you don't think about trifles, unkind thoughts won't come to your mind.

14. If you don't know about wolves, you walk through the woods without fear.
If you don't know about robbers, you are not afraid of the dark night.
If you don't know lies, it is easy to tell the Truth.
If you don't know evil, you live happily.

15. In order to find a worthy husband for his daughter, the king thought of a clever test. At the entrance to the wing of the palace where the maiden lived, they prepared a room full of various rare and precious items decorated with gold and gems. The suitors were all led into that room and told that they were free to take anything they wished but, after that, they would never see the king's daughter. Alas, the maiden was sitting alone in her beautiful chamber. No one could withstand the temptation to take something from the room.

GETTING A PRAYER

Once, a prince arrived at the palace. He was also led to the room with the gifts and offered to take anything he wished. "I do not need anything," the prince responded. "I need only to see the king's daughter." The king's courtiers showed him the way to the maiden's chamber. But at that moment, the prince noticed a very rare sword that was exceptionally sharp. He could not refrain from taking it into his hands. "So, Your Highness, you may now return home without the bride," the courtiers announced. "Not at all," exclaimed the young man! "With a sword like this, no one will be able to stop me!" So he went forward and entered the king's daughter's chamber. Amazed by such audacity, the king did not dare to refuse his request. And the king's daughter became the wife of the brave prince.

16. At dawn and at dusk the sun appears immense,
    but one can gaze at it freely.
At noon, the sun appears smaller,
    but one cannot look at it even for a moment.
Nevertheless, the sun is always the same.

When evil grows stronger, the Truth seems weak,
    but its power becomes obvious when evil weakens.
And still, the Truth is always the same.

17. He who is being pulled from an abyss by his hand must not himself let go of the hand of his savior.
He who is being protected must not himself abandon his protector.
He who is being helped must help others.
He who is being consoled must console others.

18. If you know that the marsh is deep, it is better not to go there.
If you do go, it is better not to fall into the quagmire.
If you do fall, it is better to get out right away.
If you cannot get out, it is better not to move. Maybe a way out will appear.

19. In the mountains, some young men found an old stone slab with a strange pattern. Below, were carved the words, "He who solves the secret of this pattern will become invisible and the pattern will change." They just laughed, considering the inscription to be someone's bizarre joke. But one of the young men sat down by the slab and

said that he would not leave until he solved the secret. His friends tried to convince him to abandon this ridiculous idea but he did not yield so they left. The young man stayed by the stone slab and settled there. Sometimes his friends would bring him food and leave, as the youngster was deep in his own thoughts and did not converse with them. He became thin, his hair grew long and his clothes were worn out. Once, many years later, his friends did not find him at the slab. When they took a glance at the pattern carved in stone, they noticed that it had changed.

20. A man was walking down the street with his son and met an old acquaintance. They started talking and gesturing energetically. The boy, getting bored as they were talking, looked down and saw that the speaking adults' shadows repeated their gestures. The boy pulled his father's arm, pointed at the shadows and said, "Dad, are they also talking?"

21. Among the members of an academic council there were many who loved keen debate. A visiting scientist came to read a paper. As soon as he appeared on the podium and opened his mouth, shouts of his colleagues sounded from the audience, "Incorrect! Incorrect!" The speaker had to shut his mouth. Shouts sounded again, "Also incorrect!" The speaker could not restrain himself and exclaimed, "But I have not said anything yet!" "Now this is correct," he heard from the audience!

22. It will be much better if:
You don't imagine in advance something you are not familiar with.
You don't guess in advance about something that has not yet happened.
You don't rehearse a conversation that is yet to occur.
You don't brood over a meeting with someone who is yet to appear.

23. Two young mothers with their baby carriages stopped to talk. "My little girl," the first mother said, "Already recognizes me, my husband and even the grandparents." "And my baby boy, when I come into the store with him," the second woman replied, "Always tells me himself what pacifier he needs."

24. Untethered, even a donkey tries to escape.
The pig would have run away from the butcher's knife long ago,
   but the trough doesn't let it.

GETTING A PRAYER

The drunkard would have quit drinking long ago, but wine doesn't let him.
Were it not for the grains in the snares, the bird would not get caught.

25. It is pleasant to talk about food during the time of fasting and to talk about fasting on a holiday.
It is good when a mouth eats little and speaks little.
It is good when you know and do not say.
It is bad when you do not know but say.

26. There is nothing better than a trunk, thinks the elephant.
There is nothing better than long jaws, thinks the crocodile.
There is nothing better than a long neck, thinks the giraffe.
There is nothing more useful than the head, thinks the man.

27. "Physics is something special!" says the physicist.
"Music is a great power!" says the musician.
"Nutrition is the key!" says the cook.
"Everyone will need a coffin..." says the coffin-maker.

28. It is hard for the frogs to fathom that the world is bigger than their swamp.
It is hard for the fish to imagine that beside water, there is dry land.
It is hard for the one who is asleep to realize that he is sleeping.
It is hard for a man to understand that life may not at all be what he thinks it is.

29. A lot, this is a little compared to "the most."
A little, this is a lot compared to "the least."
A lot of freedoms, this is great slavery.
There can only be one freedom, complete absence of any slavery.

30. Colorlessness, that is the true color.
Soundlessness, that is the true music.
Boundlessness, that is the true border.
Wordlessness, that is the true speech.

31. When the ignorant speak, the knowledgeable are silent.
When the knowledgeable speak, the ignorant are silent.

Mysterious Discourses

The ignorant squander and the wise keep.
The wise lose and the ignorant acquire.

32. When you abandon the pretty, you come to the beautiful.
When you abandon the good, you come to the excellent.
When you abandon the pleasant, you come to the necessary.
When you abandon the comfortable, you come to the useful.

33. Nothing comes out when:
A blind man reflects on what is the horizon.
A deaf man reflects on what is good music.
A dumb man reflects on what is oratory.
A hungry man reflects on what is the royal feast.

34. What can be said:
To someone who is looking for eternal youth,
To someone who is looking for eternal health,
To someone who is looking for eternal riches,
To someone who is looking for eternal happiness?

35. Can they stop:
A man falling into an abyss,
A man who started to hoard treasure,
A man who started to lose,
A man who loves this vain world?

36. Can you stop groaning if you have already hit your finger with a hammer?
Can you stop a quarrel if you have already become angry?
Can you stop judging others if you are already accustomed to it?
Can you stop thinking about this world if you are already dying?

37. It is good when you don't have:
A single speck of dust in your eye,
Anything greedy in your actions,
Anything insulting in your thoughts,
A single bad thought in your heart.

GETTING A PRAYER

38. Once some villagers received a gift of several pairs of sunglasses. Each pair had lenses of a different color. The people gazed at the surroundings through the glasses and argued, "Everything is beautiful when it is green! No, when it is red! No, yellow! No, blue"! A passerby heard their argument and said, "Don't you see that what you are arguing about is just colored glass? The world has nothing to do with it." "If this is the case, why are you green, red, yellow and blue," the people objected?

39. A boy asked his father, "Dad, what happens when a man dies?" "This means there is no man, son," the father replied. The boy reflected and said, "That's like in a game when I hide and they cannot find me, right?"

40. The mother tells her children that it is lunchtime but they are absorbed by their toy railway. "Boys, come to eat! Do you hear me? It is lunchtime! Are you going to come or not?!" The woman cannot stand it anymore and goes to the children's room. One of the boys raises his head and says, "Mom, it is hard to stop when the train has already departed." "For that, son, you have the red light," said the woman and stopped the game.

41. You blink once, and you are thirty.
You blink a second time, and you are sixty.
Will you have a chance to blink the third time?

A blink, and your friend becomes your enemy.
A blink, and there comes news that crashes your entire life.
A blink, and there is no one around.

42. A man who was fond of travelling dreamed of going to Egypt. Judging by books and guides, he thought it to be a country of superb delights and exalted feelings. Finally he did go to Egypt. When he returned, his friends asked him, "So, how was Egypt?" "All right," the traveler responded. "The pyramids stand but all around, there is one big dump."

43. The children play at being scouts. Whenever they notice someone from their places, they shout to him that he has been killed. The one who loses leaves the game. So someone is yelling to a fat boy, "Nick is dead!" "Wounded," he responds! Another

shout sounds, "Nick is dead!" "Wounded again," the reply comes! The children are indignant, "Nick, you were gone long ago and you are still 'wounded'!"

44. There cannot be:
Two bears in one lair,
Good without reward,
Bad without punishment,
Knowledge without selfless courage.

45. If you think that you have done something,
   it means that you have done nothing.
If you think that you have said something,
   it means that you have said nothing.
If you think that you have understood something,
   it means that you have understood nothing.
If you think that you have heard something,
   it means that you have heard nothing.

46. A farmer's rabbit ran away from its cage. It was running about the yard and would not let itself be caught. The farmer's neighbor came to help him and they started trying to catch the rabbit together, trying to corner it. The rabbit jumped into the bushes; so, the neighbor went after it. One heard the sounds of struggle and groans. Then there was silence.

"It was not easy to catch it, was it?" asked the owner of the rabbit, supposing that it had been caught. "Well, to catch it was not a problem, but to hold it, there was," replied the neighbor, climbing out of the bushes all scratched and without his prey.

47. An old professor was much loved by both his students and colleagues. But he received particular recognition after one presentation in front of a large audience, attended by several scholars whose views on the subject were different from the professor's. One after another, they remarked on the weak parts of the professor's report. By their sarcastic words, they brought the old man to a sorry state and tears were visible in his eyes. Still, he mustered up all his forces and, in a trembling voice, thanked his colleagues for their valuable remarks, promising to take into account their

corrections in revising his work. Later, as the saddened professor was walking down the corridor, various people approached to shake his hand. In their eyes, he was the true winner.

48. Two friends were canoeing down a river in the mountains. On the way, they saw a small island with a sandy beach, a pleasant meadow and some willows. "This is a perfect place to camp and fish for a while," the friends decided. They tied their boat to a willow, set up a tent, caught some trout, sat by a campfire for some time and went to sleep. During the night, they heard thunder and the sound of heavy rain. The wind was clearly strengthening. By morning, it had stopped raining but the roar of the river awakened the travelers. They looked out of their tent and realized that the rain had caused a flood in the mountains. Their boat had been carried away by the river and water was already very near. "We must get out of here fast," one of the friends said, alarmed. "How?" the other replied in frustration. "We have to swim across. Hurry"! "Oh, no," the confused man protested, "And what about our sleeping bags, our food, our tent, our money and ID's?!" "Just stuff all the papers in your shirt pocket and that's it. Let's go!" his friend replied and rushed out of the tent. He was already preparing to walk into the water but his friend was still busy with something in the tent. In a few minutes, he walked out in heavy boots, carrying his backpack. "Are you crazy?" the man standing by the water shouted. "Get rid of it all, if you want to live!" Reluctantly, his friend followed the advice and the two of them, unburdened, jumped into the stormy river. With great difficulty, struggling with the current, the friends reached the bank. They looked back and saw their clothes and the tent being carried away by the flood. The island was already submerged.

49. In one country, there was a lake in the woods and in that lake there lived an enormous serpent. As soon as people passing by the lake would think about the serpent, he appeared at once and devoured them. The serpent killed many unfortunate ones in that way. The people sought salvation but did not find it.

Once, a stranger was passing through the nearby village. He was surprised that the village seemed almost abandoned despite the fact that it was daytime. The stranger asked the villagers why they were so few and was told about the terrible serpent in the lake that devoured everyone who thought about it. "I shall give you some advice," the stranger said. "I remember that there exists a magic bird, much feared by serpents because it kills them. When you pass by the lake, think about that fascinating bird and the serpent will not harm you." The locals followed the stranger's advice and the terrible serpent left that place for good.

50. A peasant in Siberia found a gold nugget. The news quickly spread around the village. Curious people constantly appeared at the peasant's doorstep and asked him for permission to take a glance at the treasure. Some were pestering him with advice on how to sell the gold more profitably and how best to spend the money. Others were hinting that he should be very careful when he goes to the city with the gold; otherwise, he could well part with his life. The peasant did some deep thinking and finally thought of something. He came out with the nugget, put it right in the center of the square and left. His relatives were indignant. "You must be out of your mind," they said. "Why did you do that?" "Just the opposite, I am in my right mind!" the man replied. "I realized that along with the gold I found endless worry. Now I have no gold and no concerns."

51. A man liked a house that was put up for sale. He inquired about the price. "One dollar," the realtor said. "Why so cheap?" the amazed customer asked. "You see," said the realtor, "the late mistress of the house ordered that the house be sold for a minimal price if two conditions are met. First, the buyer must agree to donate a million dollars for the maintenance of the late mistress' cat and second, he must agree not to disclose the conditions of the deal. Such is the bequest." So the man bought the house for one dollar after donating a million dollars to the late owner's cat. Whenever the man's acquaintances asked him how much he had paid for such a beautiful house, he would answer, "One dollar." "What is the sense of telling such lies? This is impossible!" the man's friends reproached him. "I am telling the Truth!" he insisted, but no one believed him. Everyone came to the opinion that the man was a terrible liar.

52. If you know what you should not do, do not do it.
If you know what you should keep, keep it.
If you know what you should forget, forget it.
If you know how to live your life without thoughts about this vain world, live it.

53. Youth should prepare for maturity, not recall childhood.
Middle-aged people should prepare for old age, not recall youth.

GETTING A PRAYER

Old people should prepare for eternity, not recall maturity.
As for childhood, it is best to be itself.

54. A school student is tired of solving a math problem so he props his cheek on his hand and dreams. Now he graduates and is admitted to a university. Now he gets a Ph.D. and makes a great discovery. Now he is awarded a prestigious prize. He is standing both happy and embarrassed and everyone is applauding. The Master of Ceremonies solemnly approaches the young genius and declares, "Son, have you solved your problem? Or are you daydreaming again?" The boy comes to himself and sees that he is sitting at his desk and his father is standing by his side, smiling.

55. Is it possible to come to:
Stop thinking wrongly about life?
Stop thinking wrongly?
Stop thinking?
Stop..?

56. Why does the almond tree bloom on mountain slopes,
　　if no one sees it?
Why are there so many beautiful flowers in the meadows in summer time,
　　if no one walks there?
Why does autumn paint maple leaves in the mountain gorges,
　　if there is no one to admire them?
Why do the summits blaze so majestically under the sun,
　　if no one can reach them?

57. Can you cling to the Truth,
　　as a shipwrecked seaman clings to a fragment of a mast?
Can you stand for the Truth,
　　as a warrior stands firm, determined to sacrifice his life for his comrades?
Can you think about the Truth,
　　as a condemned man thinks about his last-minute stay of execution?
If you can, then you have hope.

58. It will be fruitless:
To ask a beggar for money,

Mysterious Discourses

To ask a deaf man for advice,
To ask a blind man to show the way,
To ask a dumb man for a reply.

59. It is undesirable:
To go astray from the first step,
To tell a lie from the first word,
To get entangled from the first desire,
To make a mistake from the first thought.

60. A master carpenter lived in the town and the residents kept him busy with their orders. Once a customer came to the carpenter's workshop during a lunch break but hardly a minute passed before he ran outside, visibly frightened. Apprentices sitting under a canopy inquired as to what had happened. "What do you mean 'what happened'," exclaimed the customer? "Your master carpenter is dead!" "Impossible!" said the apprentices distrustfully. "Before lunchtime he was quite healthy!" "I don't know how he was before lunchtime," the vexed customer responded, "But now he is lying dead in a new coffin." "Oh, there you go!" laughed the apprentices. "That's an old habit of the man. At lunchtime, he always rests in a new coffin!"

61. All manifestations of this world conceal an eternally beautiful, "Yes." But if one tries to comprehend the manifestations themselves, they will inevitably reveal that they are woven of a single miserable, "No."

62. A young man and his elderly father lived in a distant place high up in the mountains. Bored by the monotonous existence, the youth wanted to learn the meaning of life. Once a rumor reached him that somewhere in the far mountains there lived a wise man with his disciple. The young man desired to see that wise man.

Walking the roads and paths in search of the wise man, he met a village boy playing beside a stream. The young man passed by but suddenly heard a voice behind him, "Don't take this path. You need the path that is across the stream." The young man turned but the boy was not there. Hesitantly, he crossed the stream and took the path he had been told to take.

A few days later by a country bridge, he saw a girl washing laundry. The girl's radiant eyes and smile made the young man stop. His heart was possessed by the thought that he should remain in the village with that girl and stop his quest. But, remembering his decision to find the wise man, he went on. "You should take the path that begins on the other end of the village," the girl's tender voice sounded from behind. The youth turned but the girl had already disappeared.

As he continued on his way, he met a chap of the same age. They started talking and after a few minutes, the young man felt that he had found a friend. He was in doubt again, should he continue to search for the wizard or not? He stepped aside and again heard a voice, "You took the wrong road. You should turn right at the crossroads." When the young man turned, he saw that his new acquaintance had vanished.

The road finally led him to a dilapidated shack. An old man was sitting on the bench outside. He invited the traveler to stay in his house for the night. In the morning, the old man said that he was living all by himself and offered the youth to stay and live with him. "No, no," the wanderer replied, "I need to find the wise man who will explain to me the meaning of life." And he walked out of the shack. "But how are you going to find me," the old man's voice sounded, "If you are walking away from me every time?" The young man turned, but neither the old man nor his shack were there any more. "That's who appeared on my way every time," the young man realized. "In the guise of every person that I met, the wise man himself appeared to me. Now the very first person I meet shall be my teacher." And at that moment, he saw his elderly father walking towards him and the old hut in the mountains where they had lived together. Only then did the young man understand with whom he had been living and the meaning of his life was clear to him.

63. A hungry man was walking down the road and saw another man with a bundle wrapped in cloth. "It must be bread," the hungry man thought and asked, "Excuse me, what is in your bundle? Bread?" "No, these are some books that I am going to sell. I just wrapped them in cloth so that they don't get wet from the rain." "What a pity!" the hungry man said and went away.

After a while, a scientist came out of his house. He saw the man with a bundle in his arms, looking for someone on the road. "It must be books that he is carrying," the scientist thought and asked, "Excuse me, what is that? Books?" "No," the passer-by replied. "I have just met a hungry man, so I sold my books and bought bread for him, but I don't see him anywhere!"

64. Wheat fields wave freely throughout the boundless space of the earth.
Dolphins play carelessly in the quiet sea.
Swallows fly unrestrained in the clear sky.
Where is the man whose heart may easily contain all that?

65. A dialogue of a psychiatrist and his patient:
So, how do you feel?
  I think I am all right.
Do you experience personal problems?
  I think I don't.
Do your relations with family members disturb you?
  I think they do not.
What are your relations with coworkers?
  I think they are normal.
I think that you should seriously reflect on your attitude towards life.
  And I think that there is no such need.
Whatever you may think, I think that you are yet to give my words some thought,
  the psychiatrist concluded.

66. To listen to your thoughts is the same as to caress a rabid dog.
To listen to your heart's cravings is the same as to believe the advice of a madman.
To listen to your desires is the same as to trust an assassin.
He who listens to his will, unfortunately, is like the one who no longer listens to
  anybody.

67. A ladder that leads upwards has many steps.
A narrow passage inwards has many doors.
A precipice has no ladders.
A broad way has no gates.

68. He who left a prison is surprised by the abundance of light.
He who found a way out of an impassable gorge sighs with relief.
He who swam across a dangerous river admires the earth.
He who escaped from bandits is happy to be alive.

GETTING A PRAYER

69. Turn, capture it, you have never known it before, but now will know.
Touch, capture it, you have never felt it before, but now will feel.
Listen,..you have never heart it before, but now will hear.
Look...you have never seen it before, but now will see.
But, ..will you have enough time?

70. You are not falling, but there is nothing you can grasp,
You are flying, but nothing moves,
You are standing still, but the speed is dazzling,
You are not living, but it is impossible to die.

71. A ship, in order to stop, needs several miles,
A train needs several hundred meters,
A car needs several dozen meters,
A man, in order to stop, needs an entire life.

72. You cannot climb a ladder's reflection in a lake,
   but you can fall into the water from it.
You can read the words of a book, but you cannot understand everything at once.
You cannot stick to the words themselves, but you can stick to their meaning.
You can use concepts, but you cannot stick to them.

73. The words "he works" make one smile, when:
A watchman guards,
A musician plays,
A clown amuses,
A magician deceives.

74. It is good when:
In an orchestra, the drummer does not imitate the first-violin,
The cock does not imitate the nightingale,
The flies do not imitate the bees,
The man does not make his mind a dump for bad thoughts.

75. A medical board inspects a psychiatric hospital. Passing through the wards, the board members listen to the patients' questions and complaints. The most frequently

asked question is, "why did they appoint an American spy as the head physician?" Also, the patients frequently complained that, "Cold winds blow through here." After the board members finish their rounds, they make a promise to the patients. "Gentlemen, do not worry. When you recover, all your questions and complaints will naturally fade away."

76. Nothing can be told by:
An ant in amber,
A moth in fire,
A diver under water,
A sleeping man in his sleep.

Nothing can be heard by:
The one who snores,
The one who talks all the time,
The one who interrupts everyone,
The one who argues with all.

77. The young trout in a river have grown up. When they got accustomed to the surroundings and realized that they were living in a place called a river, they asked their parents, "Where does our river flow from and where to?" "Children, we don' t know from where and to where it flows. We only know that it is big and has been flowing for a long time." The youth started to worry. "And when the entire river flows out, where are we going to live?" "Don't be afraid, children," the parents responded. "The river is always with us and it will not stop flowing as long as we are alive."

78. At a reunion of adherents of different faiths, people were getting introduced to one another. "Please meet this gentleman. He is a Catholic, a formerly Orthodox." "And how did he become a Catholic?" "He was somehow offended by the Orthodox church, so he converted to Catholicism." "I see." "Please meet this gentleman. He is a Muslim, formerly Orthodox." "And how did he become a Muslim?" "You know, he was somehow offended by Orthodoxy, so he converted to Islam." "Oh, I see." "And now you are welcome to meet a Buddhist from Tibet." "You are not telling me he was also offended?!" "No, no. He is a Buddhist from birth."

GETTING A PRAYER

79. Until the dogs are thrown a bone, they wag their tails.
When scientists start to argue, it becomes clear that their reason is their biggest mistake.
The more acute an argument is, the less people understand it.
A single kind word is better than a hundred accusations.

80. A young man was invited to visit a family he knew. Everyone sat down to dinner. The young man liked gravy which was placed far from him. He threw glances in the direction of the gravy but felt too shy to ask anyone to pass him the saucer. The daughter of the hostess was seated opposite the young man and the gravy was actually standing near her. Supposing that the guest was looking at her daughter, the hostess asked him in a low voice, "So you really like what you see, don't you?" "Yes, absolutely admirable," the young man replied, having the gravy in mind. "Oh, really!" the hostess smiled. "And what do you admire most, if it is not a secret?" "Mmm...I'll tell you what exactly if you let me move closer," the young man replied.

81. Journalists often ask rock climbers to pinpoint what in particular attracts them to the mountains. Some say they are attracted by the mountains themselves. Some speak about the height or the unique views. Some prefer to stress the idea of triumph over oneself. And when the climbers' loved ones ask them whether they really think the way they say in the interviews, the climbers respond, "But we have to explain to them somehow why we go to the mountains!"

82. Only a few survive a shipwreck.
Only certain individuals climb the highest summits.
Only strong fish are able to pass through waterfalls.
Only a small number comprehend the ultimate knowledge.

83. When you are entering Moscow, there is no time to read a guidebook.
When you are running away from a bear, there is no time to look at the map.
When you are climbing the summit, it is senseless to carry a heavy load.
When the sun rises, it is senseless to read a description of dawn.

84. It is dangerous to cling:
To a woman's love,
To people's praise,

Mysterious Discourses

To a traitor's hand,
To a rotten rope,
To this world.

It is dangerous to rely:
On politicians,
On police,
On doctors,
On yourself.

85. This is a very old tale. A king told his trusted servant, "Go I-know-not-where. And bring me I-know-not-what". The servant came and brought what he had been told. The king approached, glanced and said, "You know, you had better take that I-know-not-what back there I-know-not-where." And the trusted servant responded, "It is too late, Your Majesty. It has already gotten out, I-know-not-how. And now something awaits you, I-know-not-what."

86. The ocean does not fear sharks,
The forest does not fear wolves,
The jail does not fear bandits,
The wise one does not fear unkind thoughts.

87. A singer needs to possess a voice, not a singing manual.
A single visit to a doctor is better than a dozen medical books.
A simple medicine is better than a hundred pieces of advice on how to get cured.
A counsel of an experienced fisherman is better than many fishing guides.

88. The shortest and saddest story:
A boy was anxious to finally become an adult. Then sixty years passed.

89. A single good book is better than many volumes of reviews.
A single good word is better than many good books.
A single good glance is better than many good words.
A single good smile is better than many good glances.

GETTING A PRAYER

90. If it is true that the Universe is expanding, then it must be noted that man's mind also expands. Much time will pass before it stops and begins to return into itself. But that happens very seldom.

91. A man and his son came to a watchmaker's workshop. On the walls, there were many clocks with figures of men and animals. One could see bears, hares, cocks and cuckoos. All of them were ticking, clicking, twittering, cuckooing, blinking and swinging the arms and the legs. "Dad, are they all alive?" The boy asked in amazement. "No, son," the father smiled. "Here, only the watch maker is alive."

92. It is a great pity when:
The calf runs away to the woods,
The foal, to the fields,
The child, to the street,
The mind, to this vain world.

93. Two friends were returning from the village to the city at night. On the way, they were ambushed by a gang of robbers. The friends broke loose, started running, jumped over a wall and landed in a cemetery. They hurried to hide among the monuments. The robbers climbed the wall and lit their flashlights but, failing to see their victims, went back over the wall. Their voices continued to be heard from the other side of the wall. One of the friends whispered to the other, "Listen, over here it's scary too. We had better get out." "It's all right, don't be afraid of the dead," the other man replied. "Those live ones are much scarier."

94. There lived a wealthy collector of ancient statues. A multitude of them were standing along the pathways of his picturesque park. A young student was sent to the collector with a reference from the local fine arts society so that he could familiarize himself with the amazing collection. The estate keeper reported to the Lord of the house about the student's arrival, met the guest and accompanied him across the park to the mansion. Full of curiosity, the student would stop by every statue, gaze at it and sigh admiringly. Finally, the estate keeper lost his patience, "Sir, whom would you actually like me to introduce you to, the statues or their owner?"

95. A traveler went to Rome and visited the renowned Vatican Museum. When he returned, his friends paid him a visit and asked him to tell about his impressions. Not

marked by eloquence, the man had a habit of mumbling and speaking very slowly. "Have you seen the frescoes by Michelangelo?" "Well, oh, umm..." The traveler's daughter came to his aid. "Dad is saying that the frescoes are beautiful." "And could you tell us, what are your impressions of the paintings by Leonardo da Vinci and Rafael?" "You know, umm...umm..." The daughter interfered again. "Dad is saying that they are gorgeous." "No, no, umm...excuse me, I wanted to say...umm...that at that time those halls...umm...were closed."

96. The parents celebrated the birthday of their six year-old son and all their relatives came to the party including many he had never met before. The boy was introduced to his numerous cousins, first to the older ones, then to the younger ones. After the party, all the children were allowed to play in the garden and the little birthday boy was very nice to everyone. When the celebration was over and the guests started to say their good-byes, they told the boy, "Well, it is great that you have met all your relatives. Now you know all of us. We came to love you a lot and we are ready to take you with us." But the boy clung to his mother and said, "No, I don't know you at all. I only know my mom."

97. Among the residents of one country, there existed a legend about a wonderful bird living somewhere in the mountains. The legend said that even a complete good-for-nothing, should he see the bird, could acquire great wisdom and become the king. In that country in a small mountain village, there lived a woman with her adult son who was somehow very unfortunate in all his affairs. Concerned about his future, the woman once told him with a sigh, "Oh, son, with your luck you should become the king."

The words of the woman became deeply embedded in her son's soul. Seeing that bad fortune continued to follow him, the young man decided to go on a quest for the wonderful bird. Once in an impassable thicket he managed to glimpse it but only for a moment. Scrambling back to the road, he saw madly dashing horses harnessed six-in-hand. Cries for help sounded from the magnificent carriage they were dragging. Suddenly a tall dried-up tree near the young man cracked and fell loudly, its rough branches getting entangled in the horses' harness. The horses tried to thrust forward but the tree was too heavy; so, they stopped. Pale, the king of that land emerged from the carriage, followed by his young daughter. His guards and escort were already catching up. Astonished by the unexpected delivery from a terrible danger, the king thought that the young man was their savior and took him into his service. At the palace, the young man quickly learned the etiquette and soon became renowned for his brilliant intellect and kindness. The king's daughter fell in love with him. Soon, the king held a wedding ceremony for them to which the young man invited his mother. She left her village and came to live at the palace.

98. In a city, a conference was held to which adherents of different faiths and denominations had been invited. Two Orthodox friends saw an announcement that an Orthodox priest was also scheduled to speak; so, they entered the conference hall. From the itinerary, they learned that the Orthodox lecturer was to speak in about forty minutes. One of the friends suggested staying in the conference hall to listen. But the other one objected, "It is better to go and rest in the lobby. Except for one, who else are we to listen to?"

99. A teenager came to enjoy the company of some fellows that seemed to him much more exciting than the company of his father who always scolded him. It was great fun for the boy to be among his peers. But gradually the teenager started to notice that his new friends' interests were rather primitive and their entertainment was always the same. He recalled his father's advice and realized that there was some sense to it. He decided to share his discovery with his new friends but they just laughed at him, "Get a life," they said. "Your parents are already out of date and their lectures make one sick." "Maybe their words are boring sometimes," the youth objected, "but now I know for sure that those words can be useful both in good and in bad times." He returned to his father and began to treat him with an even greater respect and love than before.

100. A family of sparrows was living under the roof of a house. When spring came, it got hot in their nest and the restless sparrow suggested to his spouse that they occupy an empty birdhouse meant for starlings. She objected saying that the birdhouse did not belong to them and that its inhabitants would soon return. The husband would not listen; so, the sparrow family settled in the starlings' birdhouse. But they did not live there long. Soon the starlings came and forced them to leave. The head of the sparrow family remembered a hollow in an old maple. But when they glanced inside, they saw a sleeping owl; so, they hurried to get away from there. The restless sparrow would not surrender. He decided to occupy an old swallows'

nest while his wife lamented that the owners would also return soon and that there would be a new scandal. And, so it happened. The swallows came back and evicted the sparrows with great noise. "You know what," the sparrow's wife said, "It is better to live in one's own nest, even if it is hot there. But in the whole world only that nest is ours."

CHAPTER THREE
HEART PURIFICATION

A rose bud can tell more about life than all the books.
An infant knows more about life than all the scholars.
A mother's heart is braver than all the brave.
A pure heart is wiser than all the wise.

1. The ocean, regardless of the coast from which one looks at it, is still the ocean. The city, both in the center and in a distant quarter, is still the city. The water of a clear spring is the same at dawn and at dusk. The heart in youth and in old age is ever deep.

2. A man went to the capital on foot. At one point, he saw an old stone pillar marking the way to the city. Around the pillar, a crowd gathered. The people were animatedly discussing in what century the pillar had been erected and during which king's rule. The traveler thought that all those people were also going to the capital; but, after listening to their conversations and arguments, he realized that not one of them had it on his mind to journey anywhere. They were interested only in the pillar itself. "And what is the distance from here to the capital?" the traveler asked. "This is also a subject of debate because the digits carved on the pillar became effaced with time." "And what direction is one to take?" "We are also trying to establish that. The arrow showing the direction is already hard to discern," they replied. "Beyond the cemetery where esteemed researchers of this pillar are buried. You may wish to visit their graves. There is some kind of road. Maybe it leads to the capital and maybe not. But if you are interested in the history of the pillar itself, you are welcome to join us and we shall further the cause of our great predecessors." "No, thank you. You may remain here with your predecessors and I shall go and try to reach the capital," the traveler said. At some distance from the pillar he met a fellow traveler and together they safely reached the city.

Mysterious Discourses

3. They say that a long time ago in one village there appeared a monster capable of changing its appearance. Thus, it would first attract people and then kill them. The residents thought of a very old man living on the outskirts of the village and decided that he could help them. The old man said that there was only one way to slay the monster. The man who has enough courage to confront it must know that the monster is capable of assuming various exteriors. Only if one holds it firmly and does not let it break loose by any means, even if it changes its appearance many times, the monster will vanish forever. Only one bold-spirited villager believed the old man. He got hold of the monster and did not let go of it until it vanished. Thus, he was able to return from his endeavor unhurt and to save the entire village from the monster.

4. A courageous youngster desired to discover something that did not exist on Earth so that his discovery would be beneficial to himself and to other people. In the far mountains, he met a gray-haired hermit and asked him whether his dream could come true. "It is possible," the hermit said, "If you follow my advice. You will enter a cave and have to undergo a serious trial. You will be asked different questions and to all of them, you shall answer, 'No.' But when you hear the principal question you shall answer, 'Yes.' If you make a mistake, you will perish."

They approached the cave. There was no one inside. But as soon as the young man went in, an imperious voice thundered, "Do you want eternal youth?" "No!" the young man responded, somewhat uncertainly. "Do you want to marry the most beautiful girl in the world?" "No!" replied the youngster even more hesitantly. "Do you want to become a renowned military commander?" "No!" the youth answered more firmly. "Do you want all the riches of the world to be yours?" "No!" he replied inflexibly. "Do you want to die for the sake of something that does not exist on Earth?" "Yes!" the young man responded with calm determination. At that moment, the ground shook and a slowly receding moan was heard, "You have defeated me. Henceforth, I shall depart from humankind." The young man turned and looked around. The cave and the old hermit were no longer there. He was surrounded by happy young people. "And what was here and left?" he asked. "Death!" they replied.

5. A rose bud can tell more about life than all the books.
An infant knows more about life than all the scholars.
A mother's heart is braver than all the brave.
A pure heart is wiser than all the wise.

HEART PURIFICATION

6. He who reaches the summit proceeds to descend.
He who dives to the depths of the sea proceeds to ascend.
He who boasts about his strength is defeated.
He who yields, triumphs.

7. He who knocks modestly at the door will surely see it open.
He who thrashes violently at the door will see it locked and barred.
He who is awaited by the master of the house will be met outside and led in.
He who is impudent and rash will see even the gates shut in front of him.

8. A man learned that in a mountain gorge there was a rock with a secret door in it. The door would not open to everyone but the man yearned to know what was behind it. So he took a sledgehammer, a chisel, a hammer, a crowbar and an axe and set out on his way. With great difficulty, he was finally able to find the door. It looked like solid rock. The man started to think about what tool he should start with. He decided to try the sledgehammer but at that very moment, the door became iron. The man reached for the hammer and the chisel but then the door turned into stone. He took the crowbar but the door immediately became wooden. The man wielded his axe and again in front of him was solid rock. Discouraged, the man collected his tools and started home. On the way, he met a traveler who was surprised by the number of tools the man was carrying on his back. When the traveler heard from the man about his unsuccessful attempt to open the door, he said, "No, you will not be able to open it like that. I have heard that if one fasts for three days in front of the door, it will open by itself. Do that and see what happens." The man followed the traveler's advice. As the third day ended, the rock, right in front of his eyes, turned into a lightly woven curtain that was gently swaying in the wind. He moved the curtain aside and went in. Then the man looked out, put his shoes by the threshold and hid behind the curtain. At that very moment, the door once again became solid rock.

9. To meet a good man during the day is happiness.
To meet his dog during the night is madness.
The yearning to gain knowledge of the Truth until old age is happiness.
The yearning to gain knowledge of the world until death is madness.

10. A city resident got lost in a forest where there lived an old monkey who possessed the gift of magic. The monkey bewitched the uninvited guest, turned him into its

slave and ordered him about as it wished. The monkey even used to ride on his neck. If the man pleased it, the monkey would sometimes treat him to a banana. The city dweller resigned himself to his fate, got accustomed to the monkey and obediently fulfilled all of its orders. One day, some hunters came to the forest. They were surprised by the sight of a monkey riding astride a man. The hunters caught the old monkey. As soon as they dragged it out of the forest, it lost all of its magic gifts. The hunters took both the monkey and the unfortunate captive to the city. The monkey was left in the zoo and the man, delivered from its charms, came to his senses and returned home. Occasionally, he would go to the zoo to look at the old monkey, wondering how it had been able to deceive him. The monkey shook its fist at the man and threw banana peels in his direction. There was nothing else it could do.

11. A young man decided to live a celibate life. Once, being too shy to speak openly about his principles, he found himself in a funny situation. Someone asked the young man if he was married. The youth, supposing that the questioning would end there, succumbed to the temptation to lie a little and said, "Yes, I am married." "And what is your wife's name?" they asked him. He had to invent something again. "And do you have any children?" another question followed. As the young man already began to lie, it was difficult to stop. "Yes, we do." "And how many?" The young man felt that he was completely lost. "Well, two," he said hesitantly. "And what are their names?" It seemed that the grilling would never end. The young man could no longer endure it. "One is named Lie, and the other is named Falsehood. I am not married. I am not!" he exclaimed.

12. You unclasp your hands, the dove flits out.
Spring sun starts to shine, the snow melts and the snowdrops bloom.
The closer you come to the edge of the forest, the more light you see.
A man's thoughts are alike to a thicket; to stay there means to be lost.

13. A dog in the yard stops the fox.
A gun in the house stops the robbers.
A sober-minded man stops an argument.
A pure heart stops bad thoughts.

14. Tourists standing on the deck of their ship started to discuss the color of the sea. "It is blue," one of them said. "No, I would say it is green," another tourist objected.

HEART PURIFICATION

"To me it seems that it is black," the third one said. The captain was passing by and heard the conversation. Failing to understand what they were arguing about, he said, "Gentlemen, this is the Red Sea."

15. Don't tease a dog and it will stop barking.
Don't argue with a rabble-rouser and he will calm down.
Don't challenge slander and it will disperse.
Don't look for excuses when you are reproached and the ones who reproach will hush.

16. The Polar star is distant, but it helps to walk the earth,
A lighthouse stands upon a rock, but it guides the ships at sea,
A map is the best adviser in a foreign land,
Don't lag behind your guide and you will get out of the thicket.

17. A snail crawls slowly, but it does not despair.
An ant is wearied by its heavy burden, but it will never throw it down.
The deeper a well is, the more water is in it.
The stronger a tooth aches, the harder it is to forget about it.

18. A boy ran into the dining room, very excited by a just-finished game with his friends. His little sister was already at the table. The boy sat down and, still recalling the game, made a horrifying face, roared at his dish and then whispered to his sister, "I am a terrible giant." The girl looked at him in amazement and suddenly burst into tears. At that moment, their mother came into the room. "What's the matter, children?" she asked. The girl pointed a finger at her brother and said tearfully, "He is a terrible...giant." "Son," the mother said sternly, "When you play you can be what you wish but at the table be yourself and don't frighten your sister. Deal?"

19. A car is speeding along a highway. The owner of the car is at the wheel and his friend is beside him. They speed past a road sign, "80 km/h" without slowing down. They pass another sign, "60 km/h." They reach a turn and suddenly see a police car. They get stopped and the driver is given a sizable fine. He gets going, visibly upset. "Did you not see all those signs?" his friend asked. "Well, I did," the driver responded, "But I have never taken them seriously."

Mysterious Discourses

20. Some close acquaintances meet for tea and start a peaceful conversation about the beauty of Switzerland. Whoever had visited that country was telling about his impressions and recalling the memorable places. An old man was sitting at the table in silence seemingly absorbed by his reminiscences. He was known to have seen many interesting places in his life, so someone asked him, "And what is your opinion about Switzerland?" "Oh yes, yes," the old man responded. "The south of France is very pleasant."

21. A boy had trouble learning the multiplication table. He complained to his father about his bad memory. "Here is what you should do," his father advised him. "As soon as you wake up, try to recall this table. Repeat it several times during the day and when you go to bed, think about it too. You must learn it so well that you are able to give the correct answers even if I wake you up during the night." "Dad, in this case I'll go to bed early," the boy said. "I am afraid I will not get enough sleep if you are going to quiz me at night."

22. During the war, a woman and her little daughter had to leave their native land along with other refugees. The tragedy and the horror of what was taking place around them were harmful to their health. Once the woman noticed that her daughter started to close her eyes during the day for long periods of time. "Are you feeling sleepy all the time, my little one?" the mother asked, alarmed. "No, Mom. I just close my eyes when I am scared. When I see nothing, I feel better."

23. A lone tree is stronger than any of the forest trees.
A blind man is alone even on a crowded street.
When a ship sinks, everyone dies by himself.
For the lone man, God is One.

24. A bad-tempered woman strongly disliked her neighbors. She took advantage of every occasion to quarrel with them. Once she made a tremendous racket over some trifle and was screaming so loudly that the entire neighborhood could hear her. The woman began insulting her neighbor very badly. He was silently doing some small work in his yard. Everyone was amazed by his patience. "How are you able to take all that so peacefully?" people were asking him. "It's all right," the imperturbable neighbor would answer. "The woman will have her say and calm down."

HEART PURIFICATION

25. Can you express what you are feeling when you see:
Starlings coming back in the spring,
Seagulls soaring over the ocean,
Swallows flying across the yard,
A mother's kind face?

26. Three Russian women and a Turkish man were traveling by train in the same compartment. Outside, as far as one could see, stretched sand dunes. The women were amazed by the barrenness and the wildness of the surroundings. They kept uttering, "How terrible is this land! How can people live here?" The train approached a little station. Behind it one could see only a few sickly trees, a camel and, further away, a mud hut. The Turkish man prepares to carry out his luggage. "You are getting out here?" the women ask, surprised. "Yes, getting out," the Turkish men answers and adds with emotion. "This is my Motherland!"

27. On her deathbed, a mother told her son about the vow she had made upon his birth. She had promised to send her first-born to serve the Great King. Now was the time to fulfill the vow. The son must reach the palace of the Great King and join the ranks of his servants. But the road there is long. It passes through a bewitched forest and the traveler will be unable to avoid various temptations and enticements. When he reaches those places, he must recall her words that will give strength to him, "Endure all, my son, and you will live."

Obedient to his mother's wishes, the young man departed. When he reached the bewitched forest, various images began to appear: beautiful maidens luring him, gold scattered on the earth, shining jewels, luxurious chariots with swift horses and chamberlains offering entrance to opulent mansions. The young man remembered his mother's words and kept going. A foreign army appeared along his way like a wall. Arrows and spears flew at him and horsemen with wild shrieks charged upon the traveler. "Endure all, my son and you will live," the last words of his mother came to his mind. The youngster went forward fearlessly and the army dispersed like smoke. Soon by the glow over the mountains, he was able to tell that the palace of the Great King was near. And at that moment, savage beasts and horrible monsters attacked the young man. They began to torment his body, tearing it with their claws and he felt the scorching heat of their breath on his face. Blood streamed from the young man's body. His forces waning, the young man again recalled his mother's words,

"Endure all, my son and you will live." Doubt enveloped his heart for a moment. Certain death was in front of him. How could he hope to live? The monsters were already roaring triumphantly but the young man collected his last strength, rose up, stepped forward, staggering, and... fell into the arms of the Great King who emerged to meet him with his servants. At that very moment, all his wounds closed as if they never existed. "I live the life which you shall also live, brave youngster," the Great King told him happily. He declared the young man his son and led him into the royal chamber. The youth served the Great King with faith and fidelity and on his gold shield, in memory of his mother, he inscribed, "Endure all, my son and you will live."

28. A man took his small son to see the Kremlin and Red Square. They saw everything and in the evening returned home, tired. The mother asked the boy, "So, son, did you like the Kremlin?" "Yes." "And the Red Square?" "The Red Square too." "And can you tell me what you were feeling when you were there?" "Of course!" the boy said. "I was feeling Dad's hand because I was afraid of getting lost."

29. For the sake of a single shot, the hunter spends the whole night in a blind.
For a fisherman, to spend the day looking at his float is true relaxation.
He who is reading an interesting book can stay awake until dawn.
If you guard your mind, the hunter, the fisherman and the reader are your teachers.

30. A young man settled overseas and decided to bring his elderly father to live with him. Experienced people told the young man that he would be able to carry out his plan only if he was lucky. When he arrived at his native country, he learned that his father had fallen gravely ill. He went to the hospital and realized that the doctors were paying hardly any attention to his father, as they saw that their patient was already very old. The young man was sitting in the hallway despondently, not knowing what to do. Suddenly an unfamiliar doctor came up to him and offered his help. After examining the patient, the doctor said that there was little hope for a complete recovery but, if treatment was to succeed, the old man could very well live a few more years. The young man, encouraged by the doctor's words, looked after his father with great care and the patient's health started to improve.

It was very difficult for a retired person to get an entry visa to the country where they wanted to go. But at that time, a new consul assumed his duties and, feeling sympathy for the young man, granted a visa for his father. Still, the old man was so weak that traveling by plane was out of the question for him. A businessman learned about the situation and, touched by the united desire of the son and the father to carry out their plan, gave them a car as a present. After studying the route, the young man realized that such a long journey in a car would also be too dangerous for his father. There remained a single possibility – to travel by ship. But there was no regular sea connection with the country they were going to. After arriving at the port, the young man learned unexpectedly that an old ship was scheduled to sail to exactly the place where he lived and that was to be the ship's last voyage. Afterwards, it would be sold as scrap metal. The father and son, as well as their car, were accommodated on board and the good doctor waved them good-bye. Reaching the country where the young man lived, they disembarked and successfully reached his home. Thanks to the good climate of the country, the young man's father recovered completely and they lived together happily for a long time.

31. A biology lesson was taking place in a school. Pictures depicting various animals were put on the blackboard but the students' attention was drawn to a cat that was climbing a tree outside the classroom window, trying to reach a nest with fledgling birds in it. "Children, attention, please!" the teacher said. "Look at the blackboard." At that moment, the cat was attacked by the aroused birds and, trying to beat them off with its paw, lost its balance and fell on the grass heavily with a scream. The students cheered and applauded. The principal was passing by and, attracted by the noise, entered the classroom. "What are you studying today?" "Cats' behavior," the perplexed teacher said. "Well, you seem to be making progress," the principal remarked and left.

32. A fisherman caught an enormous catfish. When he was already dragging his prey up to the boat, the catfish suddenly jolted the man with great force. Entangled in his fishing-line, the man fell into the water. At that moment, a shepherd was passing by on the bank. He saw the fisherman thrashing in the river and asked with surprise, "Friend, what are you doing there? Catching a catfish?" "Help!" the fisherman yelled back, "otherwise, there will be no catfish and no me!"

33. A young man fell in love with a good girl but her parents were opposed to their union. The youth could only see his beloved on the balcony of the house where she lived when she occasionally appeared to water flowers. The young man would stand beneath the balcony for entire days just to see her. The girl was touched by the young

man's fidelity and one day threw him a note, "We cannot meet because of many obstacles. Please find another fiancée for yourself." The young man threw back his own note, "For me, in the entire world, there is no one but you."

34 A lady occupied a suite in a respectable hotel. On the occasion of some holiday, there arrived in the city a large delegation headed by a person of consequence. The hotel manager, concerned with finding rooms for the members of the delegation, addressed the lady who was listening to him somewhat absent-mindedly, "We respectfully ask you to temporarily move to another room. This suite is to be reserved for a person of consequence." The lady turned to the manager and spelled out, "This. Is. Out. Of. The. Question." Then, glancing in the mirror, she added, "I am also a person of consequence."

35. A boy approached his father and asked him if he could help him to solve a math problem. The man himself was interested in the problem and began to explain it to his son with animation. At some point, he noticed that the boy, instead of listening, was swinging his foot to tease the cat that was sitting on the floor. "Son, you must concentrate on the problem," the father said sternly. However, after a while he noticed that the boy was looking out the window, drawn to a soccer game in the yard. "Son, are you able to listen to what I am telling you or not?" the father said, starting to get angry. "Yes, Dad, I am," the boy replied. "If the cat is not in the room and if they don't play soccer outside."

36. When rain pours down heavily, bubbles appear on the water.
When the waves are strong, foam covers the surf zone.
The rain will stop and the bubbles will disappear.
The surf will calm down and the foam will vanish from the shore.

37. A native of Siberia decided to try his luck at finding a job in Moscow at a television headquarters. He arrived in the capital but kept getting lost. He stopped a local person, asked for directions and was told, "Just remember that you are looking for the high broadcasting tower. If you do, you will get there for sure."

38. A visitor from the countryside entered a giant supermarket and got lost in its numerous sections. Tired of looking for an exit, he asked a salesgirl to tell him how he could get out. "This is very easy," the girl smiled. "If you don't look at what's in

the aisles but simply follow the arrows on the floor, they will lead you to the exit quickly."

39. A couple had their first baby. The husband and the wife were busy taking care of him and did not get enough sleep. One night the baby started to cry and would not calm down. The young parents did not know what to do. "Maybe he has a high temperature?" the man asked, touching the infant's forehead. "No, it seems that he does not." "Maybe his stomach aches?" the mother said, frightened. "What from?" replied the father, also alarmed. "Listen, let us call his grandmother and ask her what we should do." The baby's grandmother was asleep so they woke her up. "You didn't forget to feed him before sleep, did you?" she asked. "Oh, right, we forgot!" the baby's mother exclaimed. "So feed him and he will calm down," the grandmother said. So the problem got solved.

40. A schoolboy was weak and sickly. His peers often jeered and abused him. The boy was hurt by it but he was too weak and timid to challenge his classmates. Not knowing what to do, the boy asked his father for advice. "You should start to exercise, to lift weights and everything will be all right," the father encouraged the boy. "Well, and if I do become strong and robust," the boy objected, "and they continue to abuse me? What shall I have to do? Fight all the time." "Not at all," his father said. "When you start feeling strong, your appearance alone will stop them from disrespecting you."

41. The patient was to be administered general anesthetic before an operation. That disturbed him a lot and brought up many questions. How was his body going to take the anesthetic? Would he feel pain or would it be similar to sleep so would he feel anything at all? "You better calm down. Don't get worried," the nurse advised him. "When the anesthetic starts to take effect, you'll have your own experience very soon."

42. A boy was fond of reading good and clever fairy tales and believed everything that was in them. He was looking for miracles in everyday life but failed to find anything that was similar to his favorite fairy tales. Feeling somewhat disappointed by his quest, the boy asked his mother, "Is it all right for me to believe in fairy tales or are there no miracles in life?" "My dear," the mother answered him lovingly. "If you try to become a good and kind boy, all fairy tales in your life will come true. You

must remember that one does not look for miracles. To good people, they come by themselves."

43. A water pipe broke in the yard of a poor family. The water was oozing to the surface but the residents did not know in what particular place the pipe had burst. It was too expensive to call the plumber; so, the old master of the house asked his son to dig a ditch in order to get to the pipe. The son started digging, reached the pipe but, failing to find the damaged area, lost his spirit. "Dad, this will take forever. I have no idea how much more I'll have to dig," he complained. "Son, keep digging along the pipe and don't stop until you find where it burst. Otherwise, we'll be flooded," the old man replied. Soon they found the damaged spot and began the repairs.

44. Two friends were interested in astronomy and eagerly read books on their favorite subject. At night, they often used binoculars to gaze at the star filled sky and admired its beauty. After a while the two of them saved up some money and bought a telescope. During the day, they had studied the instructions meticulously and were eagerly waiting for nightfall. But something unfortunate occurred. Regardless of how they twisted and twirled the eyepiece, the vision of the starry sky remained blurred. "We must have missed something," the friends repeated, upset. They took out a flashlight and once again leafed through the manual. "That's where the problem is," they finally understood. "We have not wiped the protecting lens! Right here it says, 'In order to assure complete clarity the lenses should be perfectly clean.'"

45. Once there lived a good and courageous young man. He had a noble heart and was eager to help all people. That young man befriended an elder who shared the experiences of his life with him. Those conversations were always very enjoyable but one day the youth noticed that the old man started to sigh heavily. He asked about the cause of the elder's grief. "I shall tell it to you," the old man consented. He confessed to the young man that he had come to that place from the Magic City in order to help good people to reach it, but had lost his miracle-working powers and was no longer able to return. If someone were to agree to help him, they could go to the Magic City together. The young man started to implore the elder to tell him how to reach the Magic City. "That city soars over the earth," the old man replied. "It is connected to the earth by the Radiant Way that ends in a narrow gorge. Two colossal rocks close the entrance to the gorge. In order to reach the Radiant Way, one must

HEART PURIFICATION

pass between those two terrible rocks." "And how is that to be done?" the young man asked. "My son, first, you must have a brave and noble heart, yearning to help others," the elder responded. "And second, you must acquire a special ability to stop the flow of your thoughts with the aid of one magic phrase." "What is it?" the young man asked with great interest. "You must learn to repeat inwardly without ceasing the same words, 'Marvelous Lad, help me!' Then the rocks will part and we shall be able to step on the Radiant Way. But if you get troubled by a covetous thought and forget the magic words, both of us will remain here forever." "Esteemed elder, has anyone tried to help you before me?" the young man asked. "Yes, my son," the elder replied with a sigh. "But they were all rejected because of the covetous intentions with which they desired to reach the Radiant Way. The road there was closed to them forever." "I am ready to help you, Oh esteemed elder!" the young man exclaimed with vigor. From that time on, he started to devote the greater part of his time to learning how to stop his thoughts with the help of the magic phrase.

When the elder was certain that the young man had learned his lessons well enough, they set on the way to the wondrous gorge, the entrance of which was blocked by colossal inaccessible rocks. When the young man saw them, he felt doubt and wondered if it was at all possible that these rocks would move? But he chased away that thought, calling upon the aid of the "Marvelous Lad". A small opening appeared in the rocks from which there emerged Marvelous Light. The elder shook the young man's hand with encouragement. But at that moment, the youth felt the influx of the image of his beloved girlfriend whom he had wanted to marry. Her voice penetrated his very soul and it was calling him back to his native land. Unable to bear the intense pain of those memories, the youth looked at the old man and saw that he was crying, while the opening in the rocks was growing smaller and smaller and the marvelous light was slowly vanishing. "No!" exclaimed the young man. "Whatever is done, is done! I shall not retreat! Marvelous Lad, help me!" At that very moment the rocks parted with tremendous thunder and the travelers saw the Radiant Way. After stepping on it, they saw that a luminous path of the Radiant Way stretched further, down to their town, and walking that path were the young man's parents, his bride with her parents, their friends and many other people of all ages and walks of life. The young man turned, looking for the elder and, Oh miracle, instead of him was standing the Marvelous Lad. Smiling, he said affably, "I am the Ruler of the Magic City! It was me who searched so long for a brave and noble heart that would open the Radiant Way to all good and honest people."

46. A crew of fishermen was laboring on a fishing ship called "Hope." How many times per night would they throw their nets into the sea and how many times would they take them out empty while the piercingly humid autumn wind splattered salty water in their eyes. And the cold wet nets made one's hands completely numb. It was hard to even count all the tribulations. At times, the younger fishermen would start to grumble, "What is the need to do such hard work? Isn't it better to look for a job on the shore?" But the weathered fishermen reassured the younger ones, "Let us all stick to our 'Hope.' With her, we shall make a living." And indeed, after several unlucky voyages they would invariably run upon a spot abundant in fish and the large catch would be the reward for their heavy labor. The money they got for the fish was sufficient for some time and the fishermen could return to their loved ones. And then they would again put to the cold sea; but, the fishermen and their families were always provided for by their dear "Hope."

47. Once there lived an old woman with her only son. They were very poor and unhappy. The woman grew old, started to feel sick and then became very ill. The young man was taking care of her as much as he could, spending all he earned on medicine. But the woman's health continued to worsen until one day she told him, "My son, I know that there is a good king who has cures for every illness. That king sometimes walks the public road. It would be good if you meet him and requested medicine for me and happiness for yourself. But that king assumes different appearances and to recognize him is not an easy task." "So, how will I recognize him, mother?" the young man asked. "When you meet him, son, you will feel joy in your heart," the woman replied. The young man went to the public road where the good king used to pass. Trying to recognize him, he would start a conversation with everyone who was passing by but not one of those conversations filled his heart with joy. Once the young man met a very old man and, in the course of the conversation, asked him how he could find the good king. The old man responded, "The eyes of your heart must open. Without that, you will never recognize him." Then he added, "If you don't meet him here, you will not meet him anywhere regardless of how long you search." The young man politely bid farewell to the old man. When he left, the youth suddenly felt joy growing in his heart. He started running down the road in the direction where the old man had departed but he was already gone. At that moment, the young man noticed a worker digging for potter's clay. "Did you see an old man pass here?" the youngster asked him. "I am busy with my work and don't look around too often," the worker responded. "What's the matter?" "I must find the good king,"

HEART PURIFICATION

the young man responded. "And request medicine for my mother and happiness for myself. But I am still unable to meet him." "Wait, wait!" continued the young man with emotion. "For some reason talking with you brought joy to my heart, although you are a simple digger." "I have waited long for your eyes to open," the digger replied and handled him the medicine. "Remember that happiness has but a simple appearance." For an instant, the young man saw the beautiful face of the good king and the next moment, everything vanished. The young man, rejoicing, returned home and gave the medicine to his mother. She took it and was cured right away. With tears of gratitude, the woman embraced her son. "At last, happiness has come to us too."

48. To follow what your thoughts are telling you means:
To spoil the relations with all your loved ones,
To predetermine misfortune,
To prepare a big disappointment,
To lie in the grave alive.

49. A Muscovite was sent to work in a branch office of his company in the south. Whatever local points of interest he was shown, he would always say, "Well, back in Moscow we have…" A few years passed. He returned to Moscow, and on every suitable occasion would say, "Well, back in the south we have…"

50. A king constantly complained to his servants that he was feeling ill. His servants were knocking themselves out trying to please him but the king's health was getting worse and worse. A foreign doctor happened to come to their country. He examined the king and then asked his servants to leave him alone with the patient. The doctor told the king that the cause of his illness was his unhealthy and disorderly lifestyle which included eating overly abundant and luxurious dishes. The king did not believe the doctor's words. "Well," the foreigner said, "You can easily verify that I am telling the Truth. Stay alone in the forest for some time and let local peasants bring you food. You will see that I am right. The most important thing is to comprehend the cause of your illness." So the doctor departed and the king followed his advice. Simple country food made him feel much better and, away from the vain life of the court, he realized that over-indulgence had indeed been the cause of his illness. The king came to love the simple solitary life; so, he passed the scepter to his son and stayed in the forest for good.

51. If you only watch your feet, you will not see the enchanting beauty of the mountains.
On the streets of the city, you forget the beauty of the star filled sky.
At a smoke-filled dump, it is hard to recall the aroma of lilacs.
In the chase for a savings account, you forget about your soul.

52. A man frequently strolled with his dog, known for its bad temper. Whenever he walked into a neighbor's house for a chat, the dog started to bark angrily and did not stop until the master would go outside with it. The man's acquaintances got tired of that and told him, "Listen, if you want to spend some time with me, don't bring your dog along. It will not leave us in peace. Either talk to us or to your dog."

53. In the mountains, to go straight means to follow a path, regardless of how it twists.
In life, to go straight means to do your utmost to always swim against the current.
The less burdens you carry with you, the faster you come to your goal.
The more abundant is one's knowledge, the harder it is to comprehend the essential.

54. Two friends were cruising in a motorboat along the seashore. Suddenly, the motor broke down. Whatever they tried to do, it would not start. The wind and the current began to carry the boat away, towards the reefs. The weather was starting to worsen. The friends took the oars but, as the crosscurrent was rather strong, the boat was moving ahead very slowly. One of the rowers constantly put down the oars and turned around, trying to see if the pier was anywhere near. That was slowing the boat down and the other man told his impatient friend, "Let us row without stopping or else we might get caught by the storm. In that case, we will surely not make it to the shore." The friends plied their oars and soon they saw their pier to which they moored successfully and were saved.

55. Before, people desired but one,
Now they desire many things.
Before, there were brave women and men,
Now, there are buyers and salesmen.

56. It is difficult for a farmer to gather grain carried away by the mice.
It is difficult for a man to gather his thoughts scattered all over the world.

HEART PURIFICATION

It is difficult to find the center of a circle that has no circumference.
It is difficult to find a man who has found himself.

57. It is good not to let:
Mosquitoes into the room,
Flies into the kitchen,
Brawlers into the house,
Wrathful thoughts into your heart.

58. When, after a long journey, you see your home, you don't feel like visiting anyone.
Distant relatives will not replace your mother and father.
Flour, water, salt and yeast, are not bread yet.
Man, until he has found himself, is only the resemblance of man.

59. A good master will not allow:
Locusts to ravage his fields.
Birds to feed on the fruits of his garden.
Bandits to torment his wife and children.
Bad thoughts to murder his heart.

60. Even a strong man will not become a weight lifter without training.
Even for a short flight, the bird needs practice.
He who is hoping for a pardon will not plan an escape.
The heart that grasps the Truth needs no reflections.

61. If you are to be entrusted with a treasure house,
   on the way to it don't pick up the copper coins.
If you wish to listen to the warbling of the nightingale,
   don't get distracted by the croaking of frogs.
If you are looking for a spring, don't rush to drink from a bog.
Don't exchange the angelic choir for the roar of rusty pipes.

62. An infant has just been born and the mother already takes care of him.
A woodcutter fells the tree for a carpenter.
When a cook prepares dinner, he has everything necessary close at hand.
There is no knowledge yet, but the Truth is already near.

Mysterious Discourses

63. First snowflakes,
Spring sky without a single cloud,
Full moon over the forest,
Clear eyes of an infant,
All that make one think deeply.

64. In a thicket you can run into a bear.
Overgrown paths in the mountains can lead to an abyss.
A wild horse's bridle must be held tightly.
An unbridled heart has no master.

65. New life begins for:
A soldier who escapes from captivity,
A prisoner who is set free,
A patient who recovers,
A man who grasps the Truth.

66. Utmost courage is required from:
The one who is taken to be shot,
The one who is preparing for serious surgery,
The one who left the world,
The one who renounces himself.

67. What sees one off, also meets him.
What is at the start, is also at the finish.
What one leaves, he returns to.
What one gets attached to, he then runs away from.

68. A village girl came to the capital. Soon she had to face the first tribulations: the difficulty with finding herself in city life, the jeers of her female coworkers caused by the difference in their tastes and understanding of life, the inability to make the right choice and so on. She did not know what to do, whether to become the same as her new girlfriends or to remain herself, the way she was. An old relative whom the girl asked for advice told her, "My dear, you possess what the city girls don't have: frankness and ingenuity. Do your best to preserve these qualities and you will know

HEART PURIFICATION

how to do the right thing, always and in every situation. The essential thing in life is not how to survive in it but how to live it."

69. Most people do not have any riches.
Many people do not hold any rank.
A multitude of people have not won any fame.
Rare are people who can live without thoughts about riches, rank and fame.

70. Two boots started to argue. The right boot tells the left, "You are not like me. With you, everything is the wrong way round." And the left boot responds, "No, it is with you that everything is the wrong way round. And actually, I shall live without you quite fine." The master came, put the boots on, stamped his feet and said, "These are some boots for you! They make a pair!"

71. A bad habit is an unreliable aid.
Chase away the bad habit and cultivate the good one.
Good upbringing is not occasional but constant.
Constancy in good practice is life's entire foundation.

72. A little boy was afraid of the darkness. When he went to bed, he could not fall asleep for a long time. He complained to his mother about his fear. "Mom, in the darkness I don't see you and I get scared." "But you feel that your Mom is near, don't you?" "Yes, Mom, I do." "So try to remember that all the time in the darkness and you will not be afraid."

73. It is enough to see but once, to come to love:
A mountain lake surrounded by pines,
Snow-covered ridges with clouds flowing over them,
Willows with branches submerged in a pond,
People who help each other in need.

74. A man bought a speaking parrot that turned out to be very bright. The owner allowed the bird to say whatever it wanted, laughing at its remarks. Gradually he became very attached to his parrot and would tell everyone stories about it. The man's friends asked him to show them the amusing bird but in the presence of unfamiliar people, the parrot did not want to say anything. He was sitting silently in the corner

of the cage, all ruffled up. "And you told us that it was completely different," the guests said to their friend. The vexed man told his bird, "Jack, tell us something." "Fools!" the parrot cried. "You see!" rejoiced the man.

75. Everyone's idea of life is different:
The mosquito's: "Blood or death."
The bear's: "The honey of the bee-garden belongs to everyone."
The wolf's: "Life requires sacrifices."
The frog's: "Our swamp is the best in the world."

76. Until the bucket is lowered into the well,
   the sky reflected in the water will not be disturbed.
Until a burst of thunder sounds, the silence of the mountains,
   it seems, will last forever.
Until footprints appear upon a snowy glade, it is like a single whole.
As long as the heart takes in bad thoughts, it has not fallen away from life.

77. Until you look inside the hollow, you wouldn't believe that the tree is coreless.
Until you walk into the cave,
   it is hard to imagine that there could be such cavities in the mountains.
Until you sail the sea, it is impossible to comprehend its real size.
Until you enter the heart, it is impossible to grasp its depth.

78. If currency has been examined by the bank, they don't cause concern.
If a man has been tested in hardships, you trust him in everything.
If the word is verified by life, you believe it fully.
If the Truth is revealed, all doubts vanish.

79. A group of tourists were traveling in Spain. One of them exclaimed with surprise, "Look, far on the right, there's a huge bull!" "Where? Where?" the curious tourists started to ask one another. "Over there on the hill, a black bull!" When the bus approached the hill, upon which the strange bull was standing, everyone realized that it was not a real animal but a plywood board in the form of a bull – a symbol of the Spaniards' love towards those powerful creatures. Further along the road, the tourists noticed some other huge figures, "Look, some more bulls! And some more!" they shouted. And one man underscored with irony, "Plywood ones!"

HEART PURIFICATION

80. A man went into the mountains to hunt partridge. Crossing a meadow, he scared off a few birds after almost stepping on them. The partridges flew away with a loud cry so fast that the hunter did not have time to even pull the gun off his shoulder. Vexed by his blunder, he took the gun in his hands. At that moment, three more partridges flushed a few steps away from him. The hunter did not expect that and had no time to take aim. Holding the gun in readiness, he started to carefully examine the grass. About ten minutes passed but nothing moved. There was complete quiet. Lowering the gun with disappointment, the hunter stepped forward and at that moment an entire family of partridges flushed right from under his feet. The surprise made him miss the chance again. "But what is that! Such crafty creatures!" the hunter exclaimed angrily, assuming that all the birds were already gone. The sound of his voice scared off a huge flock of partridges that was hiding in the grass behind him. The flock took wing and sped away down the gorge. The hunter angrily aimed his weapon and fired but it was already too late. On that day, he failed to shoot a single bird.

81. Do you want to comprehend this world? Everything inevitably recurs in it:
From morning until evening,
From the beginning of the year until its end,
From birth until death,
From the beginning of the world until its end.

82. A desert hare, a Siberian camel, an African bear and an Australian lion met a man. He asked the hare how it had adjusted to life in the hot sands. The hare told him that it had become two-humped, had learned to live without water and to feed on thorns. The Siberian camel told the man that it had learned to bury itself in the snow, feed on moss, run fast and cover up its tracks. The African bear said that it was now able to hide from the hunters in the depth of the jungle and to eat mangoes. The Australian lion said that it was now hunting kangaroos and scaring away the aborigines by its roar. The man asked them, "And why did you actually come to me?" "We want to be friends with you." "Why?" the man wondered. "Because we are your thoughts," the beasts replied.

83. A farmer bought a piglet and put him in the pigsty. The animal turned out to be very active. Very soon, the piglet dug under the supports that were propping up the pigsty and it became so lopsided that the farmer could hardly enter. Then the piglet

climbed out of its pen and dug up the whole yard. The farmer was dazzled by such activity and would not stop the restless animal. After the pigsty, the piglet dug under the summer kitchen. Its walls started to crack and it was barely holding up, so the farmer had to prop it up with poles. The piglet was now busy digging under the foundation of the farmer's house. The neighbors, seeing all the damage the animal was doing, were trying to convince its owner to stop the destructive work of the pig (which, it must be noted, had already grown bigger and stronger). But the farmer responded that he enjoyed the vigorous activity of that creature. "Poor fellow," the neighbors said with sympathy. "If you don't stop this 'vigorous activity', you will soon have nowhere to live!"

84. A man liked to drag to his house whatever was at hand. If someone threw away a broken armchair, the man would take it home. After all, it could still be of use. If someone got rid of a broken bucket, the man would also take it thinking that he might need it one day. Soon, there was no free space left in his rooms. The entire house was full of "useful" items.

Once, a tap started to leak in the man's kitchen and he had to call a plumber. "Give me something that I can sit on," the plumber asked. "Please, here is an armchair," the master of the house said, offering him a broken armchair. "You'd be better off throwing it out the window," the plumber grumbled. "And give me a bucket so that the floor doesn't get wet." "Please," and the man handed him a broken bucket. "You know what you should do with this bucket?" the vexed plumber asked. "No." "Let it accompany your armchair."

85. It was wartime but there was no active combat. The hostile armies dug in and limited themselves to regular exchanges of artillery fire which started and ended at the same exact time every day. The shells were causing much damage to residential areas and taking the lives of numerous civilians. There came a time when a local resident decided that on that particular day, the artillery duel would not take place. When the usual time of the exchange of fire approached, he was calmly working near his house, repairing a broken fence. A neighbor, heading for shelter, shouted to him, "Hey, friend! Put everything down and run to the shelter! Any minute, they will start to fire!" "And maybe there will be no shooting today?" objected the man, reluctantly interrupting his work. "Listen, you have no time left already! You must get in now! They will fire, and you will either save yourself or die!"

HEART PURIFICATION

86. A man went on vacation to Cyprus. From there, he called his relatives back home but the connection was poor. The traveler said that he was in Cyprus. "Where? Where?" they asked him. "In Cyprus!" he shouted into the receiver. "Cyprus, where Aphrodite was born!" "Who, who was born?" the relatives asked again. "Aphrodite was born!" the man shouted loudly. "Oh, now it's clear!" responded his relatives. "Please congratulate the baby's parents on our behalf!"

87. A large family is sitting at the table. One of the relatives living in the house walks in. "Oh!" he says and sits down. "What's wrong with you?" they ask him. "I have a headache." "We feel for you," voices say. "Is there any medicine at hand?" "Yes." "Well, get better." The next day the same relative again sits down with a moan. "What's wrong with you this time?" other family members ask with sympathy. "Headache again?" "No," the man replies with a sigh. "This time, the small of my back hurts." "What a pity!" the relatives say. "Do you have any medicine?" "Yes." "We wish you to recover quickly." "In the morning, the sick man comes for tea and moans again while sitting down. "What happened? The small of the back again?" "No, the headache returned," replies the man. Everybody is confused. Then someone says, "We wish you to get rid of all the illnesses that you may have!" "I have, I have!" the sick man says gladly. "I see that you are feeling for me, so I took along the list of my illnesses and will now read it to you!"

88. A wild duckling climbed out of the egg and was surprised, "I can walk!" When he followed the duck to the water, he was surprised and gladdened even more, "I can swim too!" And when the duckling grew up and became stronger, he realized that he could even fly. But even that was not all. He made another discovery. Not only could he fly above his pond but he could cross great seas and reach unknown distant lands.

89. If the morning sky is dull, maybe you should just rub your eyes?
If all your loved ones look displeased,
   maybe it is because you are displeased with something yourself?
If people seem stingy, maybe it is because you are the scrooge?
If something in life does not go right,
   maybe it is because something is not right inside of you?

90. In the high mountains, there is nothing except the mountains.
In a clear spring, there is nothing except pure water.

Mysterious Discourses

In a kind character, there is nothing except kindness.
In a pure heart, there is nothing except God.

91. Freedom is deeper than what they think it is.
Freedom is grander than they imagine it.
Freedom is more valuable than life itself.
Freedom is not at all the way it is understood.

92. A hunter was passing the winter in a small hut. Once he sat on a stool by the window, took out a needle and started to thread it. But the needle slipped from his fingers and fell. That was the only needle he had. To lose it would be a pity; so, the hunter started to look for it on the floor. It was nowhere to be found. He moved the stool away but still he could not see the needle, maybe under the bunk? He kneeled and crawled there but to no avail. Probably it is under the table? He looked and looked but saw nothing. Maybe by the door? He searched and searched. The needle was not there either. The hunter grew tired and quit searching. He just sat down on the stool to rest. Lo and behold, the needle was there! Just lying by the stool's leg and that was it. "Eh! Had I known, I would not have searched for such a long time!" the hunter exclaimed with regret.

93. In a village there lived a young man. For entire days he would sit at home and do nothing. Once he asked his mother, "How can I find happiness?" "Son, go out into the open, whatever you catch will be your happiness," she replied. The young man went out into the field and saw a foal. He rushed to catch it but could not. A hare jumped out of a bush. He rushed to catch it but could not. Then he saw a dove flying. He rushed after it, but it was useless. It flew away. The youngster looked and saw a crow walking on the field, searching for worms. There was nothing left for him but to reach for the crow, so he caught it. "Is it possible that you are my happiness?" he asked. "No," responded the crow. "What kind of happiness am I? But I could tell you how to catch happiness." "How?" the young man asked. "Take some fragrant hay, put it by your yard. The foal will come to eat hay and will remain with you. Take some sweet carrots, put them under the fence. The hare will come, see the carrots and it will become completely tame. Throw some grains of wheat about the yard. The dove will come and settle under your roof." "Is that all there is to happiness?" wondered the young man. "And happiness will come next. When a kind and beautiful

girl walks by your yard, she will see how you feed the foal, the hare and the dove, fall in love with you and become your wife."

94. When wind penetrates the house, close the doors tighter.
When frost grows stronger, heat the stove better.
When mice are in the house, search for their burrows.
When bad thoughts approach the heart, look for the gaps in it.

95. A young man decided to pay a visit to his neighbors. He was met by a middle-aged man who introduced himself as a brother of the master of the house. The neighbors themselves were still at work. The neighbor's brother started a conversation with the guest. He began to tell about himself and about his problems, the essence of which was difficult for the young man to grasp. However hard the guest exerted himself, he was unable to understand anything. Soon he was completely at a loss as to what was the case in point. At that time, the neighbors came home. When they saw that the young man was conversing with the host's brother, they just grinned and said, "What made you start talking with him? The man has just been discharged from an insane asylum. Has he not warned you? Or can you not see it yourself?"

96. A man was walking in the mountains and saw a scorpion on a stone. It lifted its tail, as if to greet the man and they started to talk. The scorpion said that it was living there not alone but with its good friend. "And where is that friend of yours?" the man asked. "There, right behind you," the scorpion answered. The man turned and saw a snake. The snake raised its head and started to hiss. "Why is it hissing?" the man asked. "It wants to greet you!" the scorpion explained. My friend is very courteous and so am I. When I want to sting, I raise my tail and when the snake wants to bite, it hisses."

97. A young man was walking down a city street. He noticed a small pocket-sized book on the ground, got curious, picked it up and started to leaf through it as he went on his way. At that time, screams sounded and people began to rush about the sidewalk. An old two-story building that had been prepared for demolition collapsed with great noise. The young man was passing near and came very close to getting hit by the crashing wall but he was absorbed by his reading and did not even notice the terrible danger he had barely avoided. As he walked up to an intersection, brake

sounds were heard. A beautiful sports car, trying to make a steep turn, wheeled onto the sidewalk, overturned and started rolling in the young man's direction. Another instant and the car would have crushed him. But it hit a concrete post and, after overturning for the last time, remained lying upside down. The young man was saved but, carried away by the book, did not even notice it. Having made a turn, the young man approached a construction site. Something crashed above. The scaffolding started to fall down, threatening the lives of all who were near the building. Passers-by were scattering in all directions. Iron pipes and wooden planks were falling around the young man with thunderous noise. But, entirely immersed in his reading, he did not see or hear anything. Fortunately, nobody was hurt. The young man approached his college hall, finished reading the book and shrugged his shoulders, as he did not find anything worthwhile in it. The title of the book was, "Three wondrous ways to escape death."

98. A sinking ship is saved through any means.
The strongholds of a city are defended to the end.
In spiritual warfare, there is no mercy for captives.
As hard as it may be, there is no way of retreat from the heart.

99. He who is falling from a precipice is trying to catch hold of something, anything.
He who is in water is doing his best to swim out.
He who is dangerously ill is clinging to life as long as he can.
But he who has yielded to bad desires and thoughts must undertake even greater efforts to stay on the way of good.

100. It is good when you are not afraid of anyone.
But it is better when no one is afraid of you.
It is good when everyone loves you.
But it is better when you love everyone.

Chapter Four
Controlling the Mind

If a man unceasingly thinks about the Truth:
As a child thinks about his mother,
As a youth thinks about his beloved,
As a mature man thinks about his wife and children,
Then such a man will undoubtedly comprehend the Truth.

1. In a dangerous place, wherever you may be, it is best to stop and look around.
In any quarrel, however far it may have gone, it is best to stop and ask for forgiveness.
In bad deeds, regardless of how many of them you may have done,
   it is best to stop and make penance.
At any age, regardless of how long you may have lived,
   it is best to stop and think about life.

2. The northern coast of one island was a zone of high humidity and people there suffered greatly from dampness. Once, some tourists came to the island. They struck up a conversation with the locals who started to tell them about the excessive humidity in that area. Even new nails, if they are left outside for the night, get ruined. The nails become rusty and are good for nothing. Another local joined the conversation and, having learned what it was about, added, "That's right. But this dampness of ours can do something that is even worse. If you forget a box of nails in the yard, in the morning you will find neither the box nor the nails."

3. A king had two sons. They had different characters but the king loved both of them. The older son was keen on hunting and the younger son came to like gambling. Their infatuations soon developed into passions. The older son hunted less to look after the affairs of the state that the king had entrusted to him and the younger son kept losing his father's money. The king became angry and ordered the older son not to go hunting at all and not to give the younger son any money for gambling.

Mysterious Discourses

The older son harbored a grudge against his father and stopped talking to him. But the younger son repented. Ashamed of his behavior, he fell on his knees whenever he saw his father and repeated, "Father, forgive me!" The king was touched by his younger son's repentance and again took him into his confidence, having bound him by a promise not to indulge in vices any more. The older son continued to proudly keep silent and nursed a grievance against his father; so, the king sent him away as an ambassador to a distant country saying, "He who does not take offence will not be offended. And he who bears a grudge will also bear his punishment."

4. A husband and wife who used to be well off grew poor. They had to sell almost all their furniture and expensive things. "How empty it looks now," the wife said in distress. "It is frightful. How are we going to live?" The husband comforted her. "It's all right, we'll get by. And look how cramped the house used to be because of all the furniture and now there is so much light, so much air and so much free space." "You are right," the wife sighed. "It remains only to grow accustomed to the free space in our wallet."

5. A powerful and peace-loving king had a favorite advisor who fell ill and died. It was announced all over the country that the king was looking for a new advisor. A multitude of people gathered under the windows of the palace. The king decided to test the candidates so that he could select the one who was worthy to become his advisor. He gave his servants an order to pour water on the waiting candidates. Those who were insulted by such treatment hurried to get away. Only one man continued to stand under the window completely unperturbed. "It looks like we have found the one we need!" said the surprised king. "But we shall put him through one more trial. Go and curse him out well." The servants brought the candidate into the courtyard and began to swear at him, calling the man a miserable good-for-nothing and a lunatic who imagined out of pride that he was worthy to be the king's advisor. "Well, if I am unworthy to be an advisor," the man responded calmly, "I shall leave. You can convey this to the king." After hearing that response, the king went to the man and said, "I am appointing you an advisor by my royal decree but first tell us who you are and what you are? And how you were able to withstand all the insults with such patience?" "Oh, Great King! I used to be an advisor of your enemy who was preparing to attack your kingdom. I was trying to dissuade him and for that I had to suffer indignity and insults every day." "And why were you trying to dissuade your king from attacking my kingdom?" "Because it is impossible to triumph over a state

that has many friends and does not attack its neighbors. He who treacherously prepares for war is overcome by the stronger one. So, it happened. Now, neither our king nor the kingdom exist and the residents have been taken captive." "And how were you able to escape?" "I assumed the appearance of a madman. And therefore all the insults and humiliations mean nothing to me." "You are able to be a madman, and that is why you are wise," the king concluded.

6. He who reaches out but to pick a flower is taken captive.
He who turns in order to look back may stay there forever.
He who laughs will not notice when his hair becomes gray.
He who doubts dooms himself to a life amidst disappointments.

7. It is fruitless:
To sow seeds on stony ground.
To sow seeds on good ground where rain does not fall.
To sow seeds on good ground where rain does not stop.
To sow seeds on good ground where rain is moderate but where weeds ruin all the sprouts.

8. He who does not listen will not learn.
He who does not practice will not understand.
He who does not live by what he has learned will not master.
He who does not become what he has mastered will not pass on the knowledge to others.

9. A high mountain is silent, but people talk about it.
An elephant does not trumpet its own force, as it is obvious.
However a mouse brags about its courage, it escapes from a cat at full speed.
However proud thoughts may put on arrogant airs,
　humility disperses them as sun disperses fog.

10. When there is something to say, it is better to speak simply.
When there is something to hear, it is better to keep silent.
When there is something to see, it is better not to look elsewhere.
When there is something to learn, it is better to forget everything you know.

Mysterious Discourses

11. You let the pigeons go and they will come back to the pigeon loft.
You untie a dog and by evening it will return to the kennel.
You chase the pigs to the field and by night they will return to the pigsty.
For the bad thoughts, let the heart be neither a pigeon loft, a kennel or a pigsty.

12. When you are standing in the center of Red Square, there is no need to ask the way to the Kremlin.
Everything you have read about the sea is nothing compared to the feeling that embraces you when you see it.
The novels that you read in the time of your youth are useless in old age.
Great goals remain great all your life.

13. If there is no feed in the lake, neither will there be fish in it.
If there is no forest in the district, neither will there be bears around.
If a man is modest, his friends are similar.
If the heart is pure, happiness finds it itself.

14. When they start to prepare dinner, there is a lot of noise and many questions.
As dinner is being cooked, there is less noise and fewer questions.
When dinner is ready, there is neither noise nor questions any more.
When the heart is ready, true knowledge comes to it.

15. A boy asks his father, "Dad, what is the Aurora Borealis like? Like the sun?" "No, son." "Like the moon?" "No, not like moon." "Like a floodlight?" "Not at all, son." "Maybe it is like a light bulb?" "No, not like a light bulb." "Dad, in this case I cannot even imagine what it is like." "Yes, son, only when you see the Aurora Borealis yourself will you understand what it is like."

16. A man and his son are working in the yard. The father says, "Son, go to the workshop and bring the big hammer here." The son leaves and does not come back for a long time. The father shouts, "So where is the hammer?" "I don't see it, Dad!" "Turn everything over and find it!" the father says. Again a long silence follows. Finally, the man asks again, "When are you going to bring the hammer?" The son emerges from the workshop, completely dirty, and says, "Dad, I turned everything over but I still can not find the hammer." Both of them go to the workshop. Indeed, everything is turned upside down. The man says gloomily, "Look, there is the

hammer, right on the wall. And you have really turned everything over." "But this is what you ordered, Dad!"

17. A girl is sitting at the dinner table. She is spoon-feeding her doll and saying, "Eat the porridge, eat, my little one." The girl's mother interferes, "Dear, please leave the doll alone and eat yourself because the doll does not eat." "Yes, Mom," the girl replies, "I know that the doll does not eat but we played together and she got hungry."

18. A youngster came for advice to an old wise man. As they were talking, he remarked, "Take me, for instance. I don't drink. I don't smoke. I don't do anything bad." "Nothing at all?" "Nothing." "So you are a saint?" "Well, almost." "And what bothers you then?" "You see, I argue with my mother a lot."

19. If a man unceasingly thinks about the Truth:
As a child thinks about his mother,
As a youth thinks about his beloved,
As a mature man thinks about his wife and children,
Then such a man will undoubtedly comprehend the Truth.

20. A woman wrote a letter to her brother living in another city and invited him to visit her. She wrote her address, "Front Street." As the brother was thinking it over and planning the trip, a year elapsed. The woman sent another letter, in which she warned her brother that her street had been renamed and was now called Main Street. After some more procrastination, the brother finally went. He started to look for Main Street but it turned out that there were several streets with such a name. He walked through all of them but his sister's house was not there. The man started to ask passers-by for directions but no one was able to help him. Finally, he met a man who surmised, "It is the street that used to be called Front Street, isn't it?" "Yes, exactly!" "You need to go in this direction." The visitor went where he had been told but came to a wrong street again. He began asking people, "Where is Main Street, formerly known as Front Street?" Someone replied to him, "There is no more Main Street anymore. Recently it was renamed again. Now it is called Fairview Street. Perhaps I can guide you there?" "No, thank you!" the man responded. "I better run there quickly before it gets renamed again."

21. A peasant had a dream that he was dying of thirst. He was dreaming that he ran out into the yard and began looking for the well but it was not there. How could he live without the well? The peasant clutched his head in despair…and woke up. "But a well must still be dug. How is one to live without a well?" he thought, being still half-asleep. So he took a spade, went to the vegetable garden and started digging. No, he realized, there would be no water there. He went out to the field but, over there, water was so much more out of reach. Then the man remembered, "By the old pear tree there was a fine place for digging." So he went to the old pear tree and the well was already there. It had been dug a long time ago by his father and the water in it was good. The peasant drank some water and washed his face and felt such joy and peace in his heart! "Here's the point!" the peasant thought. "You just have to wake up well and truly, that's all."

22. A boy was taking a walk on the street. Suddenly he heard someone calling him. He turned and saw a decrepit old man throw a beautiful multi-colored ball to him. He stretched his hands to catch the ball but while the ball was flying, the boy finished school, graduated from college, got married, his children grew up, he buried his parents, became old himself and his hands became weak and wrinkled. When the old man caught the ball, he was already unable to hold it in his hands. Then he noticed another boy, running merrily along the street. The old man called to him and, with his last bit of strength, threw to him the beautiful multi-colored ball of childhood…

23. A man went to Rome, Italy. In order to reach the Coliseum, he had to take the metro. On the wall of the metro car he saw a sign, "Beware of pickpockets." And then he had an idea. He took out a new notebook, wrote something on its first page and put it in the side pocket of his jacket. As the train approached the center of the city, more people came into the car and it got crowded. The man felt someone's hand slowly going into his pocket. But he only smiled and pretended that he did not notice anything. As the train came to the next stop, he noticed that one of the passengers was standing nearby with his notebook in his hands and looking at its first page with surprise where it was written in Italian, "Sorry, there is nothing in the pocket." Their eyes met and they understood each other without any words.

24. Once a young man went on a date with a girl but when he reached the agreed upon place, it started to rain so heavily that he got completely soaked. The young man decided to be true to his word and did not leave. Only one thought disturbed

CONTROLLING THE MIND

him, "Can anyone at all come in such weather? If she comes, it will probably be like a miracle." The girl came to the date in that terrible rain, also completely soaked, although she had an umbrella. Many years have passed since then. But every time they remember that evening, it was as if they became twenty-year olds again.

25. Stars glitter above the dark tops of the cypress trees, the fragrance of jasmine fills the gardens, nightingales sing in the blackthorn bushes. In these first nights of May, white lilies bloom. How alike they are to the hearts of people who lived here a long, long time ago...

26. If you get lost in a thicket, do not hesitate to look for the road.
Even a fly in a cobweb can set itself free, if it does not hesitate.
The stronger the current of a river, the faster you must get out of it.
The less time you have, the more decisively you must act.

27. A bandit will not cleanse himself of dirty deeds by bathing in a clear spring.
A thief will not become better by stealing from good people.
A politician will not become more honest by pretending to be a decent person.
The heart cannot be called pure, if even one bad thought remains in it.

28. The cat slumbers calmly, but it hears clearly the rustle of a small mouse.
Before the dolphins start their play, the sea appears deserted.
For the ocean, even a whale is a tiny fish.
The pulsation of one heart resonates in every little corner of the universe.

29. They like to say about themselves:
A scrooge: "I am thrifty."
A squanderer: "I am generous."
A boor: "I am brave."
A traitor: "I am truthful."

30. To comprehend others and not to comprehend yourself means to lose both others and yourself.

31. A king among men,
   is dust before God.

Mysterious Discourses

A man alike to a king before God,
  is dust among men.

32. Water does not penetrate a sturdy boat.
Gadflies do not sit on a running horse.
A laboring man has no time to dream.
He who watches his heart does not sink into idle thinking.

33. Autumn rain pours outside, and the man snuggles up in his warm room.
Thunder sounds far away, the housewife hastens to take the laundry from the clothesline.
For the one who is afraid of bandits, all people are crooks.
But for a small child, the entire world and all people are good.

34. For a hungry man, bread is more valuable than gold.
He who is in despair can be helped by a single kind word.
He who is in trouble needs at least one true friend.
He who is searching for the Truth will not be attracted by anything else.

35. It is no wonder that a beetle creeps,
  but it is amazing that it can fly.
It is no wonder that a man loves another,
  but it is amazing that he can love all people.
It is no wonder that a man fights for his life,
  but it is amazing that he can sacrifice it.
It is no wonder that a man can think,
  but it is astonishing that he can comprehend the Incomprehensible.

36. To caste bells and to gild the domes of churches,
  is good but it is still far from Love.
To build churches and to raise monasteries,
  is even better and it is already close to Love.
To comfort children, old folks, sick people and prisoners,
  that is very near true Love.
To help at least one suffering person all your life,
  that is genuine Love.

CONTROLLING THE MIND

37. The more you chase away mosquitoes with your hand,
    the more of them fly to you.
The more you wave a stick at a dog, the angrier it gets.
The more you look for excuses, the more accusations emerge.
The more offensive words you say, the more insults you hear.

38. A man is preparing to go on a business trip and is talking to himself, "Did I take a towel? Yes. Did I take a toothbrush and toothpaste? Yes. Slippers..." His wife shouts to him from another room, "Did you take clean shirts?" "Yes," the husband replies. "Well, where did I stop? A towel? Yes. A toothbrush and toothpaste..." "And did you take a spare tie?" "Yes, yes!" the man yells back. "Okay, one more time. A toothbrush and toothpaste? Yes." "And slippers?" the wife shouts again. "Yes, yes! Don't disturb me, otherwise I'll really forget something!"

39. He who has forgotten about joy, does not grieve.
He who has forgotten about health, does not fall ill.
He who has forgotten about old age, does not grow old.
He who has forgotten about life does not die.

40. A young man came to get hired for a job. His acquaintances already spoke with the director of the firm on his behalf. It only remained for the young man to go and talk to the director himself whenever the latter had free time. But that day, the director was very busy and did not leave the conference room. The young man kept asking the employees what their boss looked like and what the best way to address him was. Everyone was showering him with advice and explaining what the director looked like. The youngster was completely confused. He was in doubt whether or not he would be able to recognize the director when he walked out of the conference room. Then an experienced secretary told him, "Young man, why are you so distressed? When people start to emerge from the conference room, you will recognize the director right away. So stop fretting."

41. A beast does not charge someone who looks it bravely in the eye.
A mature man is devoid of childish fears.
A snake-catcher is never afraid of snakes and scorpions.
A courageous soul breaks the slavery of the mind as a lion breaks a cobweb.

Mysterious Discourses

42. For man, happiness is to be healthy.
An even greater happiness is to be healthy and handsome.
A much greater happiness is to be healthy, handsome and rich.
True happiness is to be spiritually free from all of the above.

43. He is alike to a madman:
Who gathers rubbish on the streets and carries it to his house.
Who gathers stones from wastelands and casts them in his field.
Who gathers gossip amongst people and collects it in himself.
Who consents to bad thoughts and keeps them in his heart.

44. He who has tried honey does not care for sugar.
He who has gotten out of a quagmire will not be driven into it again.
He who has foresworn the world will not be held by anything in it.
He who has mastered true knowledge will not be forced to renounce it.

45. In order to be free of all worries, you should learn:
To place no value on your desires,
To place no value on your thoughts,
To place no value on the entire world,
To place no value on your own self.

46. Even if all the money is divided equally among all people,
   very soon some will have more of it than others.
If all knowledge is divided equally,
   very few people will be able to take advantage of it.

47. Without patience, a mosquito will seem like a ferocious beast.
With patience, you will tame even a rabid bull.
Without patience, a mouse will seem like a tiger.
With patience, mountains and seas will part.

48. A house without a foundation will not stand long.
A wall without mortar will not hold long.
Will without power is the source of all troubles.
Mind without prayer is an excruciating nightmare.

CONTROLLING THE MIND

49. A snake cannot lurk on a public road.
A flea cannot hide in a white garment.
A wasp cannot survive for long in a room.
Vanity cannot be obscured by a hypocritical smile.

50. Near a big city there are big dumps.
The larger carrion is, the stronger its stench is.
The higher the rank is, the more pride there is.
It is better to stay away from a proud man, like it is from carrion.

51. A soldier rejoices to be alive after a battle.
A greater joy is to break out of confinement.
An even greater joy is to escape from captivity.
But the true joy is to gain eternal life.
To break out of the confinement of passions.
To escape from the captivity of the mind.

52. In the Caucasus, the Bolsheviks arrested a group of the Orthodox faithful. The people were told that they would be shot early in the morning. For the night, the detainees were locked up in a large, cold shed. A youngster heard an old man beside him begin to speak. "Listen to me all!" the old man said. "I know that the Bolsheviks will have our hands tied and take us to the steep river bank to be shot just as they have done before with others. Right before the order, 'Fire!' is heard, I will rush forward. The soldiers will hurry to shoot me and you should all jump into the river. If you stay alive, try to get close to the bank. That way it will be harder for them to notice you. The rope will loosen in the water and you will be able to free your hands." "Grandpa, let us all jump into the water together," the young man started to entreat him. "No, son," the old man responded calmly, "Someone must distract them. My life is over in any case and you may still save yourself." However the youth pleaded, the old man persisted with his intention.

Early in the morning, all of the faithful had their hands tied. They were brought to the steep bank and the sound of the mountain river could be heard below. At the command, the soldiers shouldered their weapons and prepared to shoot. The old man rushed forward and shots sounded. The young man jumped into the river, feeling that a bullet had hit him in the shoulder. He found himself in the water and other people were falling down close to him. With an effort, the youngster managed to free his hands. Gasping for breath and choking, he began to swim towards the bank. The river current itself carried him to a spot under the precipice where he was able to cling to the roots of a tree. Shots, screams and curses sounded from above. The soldiers were trying to see if anyone had swum out. But there was no one in sight so they left. In spite of the pain in his shoulder, the young man climbed out onto the bank. Some locals picked him up and treated the wound that turned out to be superficial, as the bone had not been hit. The young man survived. He always remembered with deep gratitude the old man who had sacrificed himself so that he could live.

53. A man settled in the woods of the Caucasus, in seclusion. He frequently met wild animals on the forest paths. The hunters warned him that it was dangerous, particularly the encounters with bears. They gave the man a flare pistol, so that he could scare the animals away in case of danger.

Once, in the beginning of the winter, the man decided to take a walk in the forest. With a loaded flare pistol in his pocket, he set out on his way and walked some distance away from his hut. He was admiring the clear forest, illuminated by dim sunlight and blue sky, shining through the crowns of larches. After climbing a hill, he looked downwards and noticed a she-bear with a cub, digging in some fallen leaves. The she-bear heard the sound of steps, looked upward and charged the man with its teeth bared. Dumbfounded, he was only able to exclaim, "Lord, have mercy!" The she-bear did not expect to hear a human voice. With a roar, she turned back and ran away towards the ravine along with the cub. Still struck with fear, the man put his hand into the pocket of his jacket and found the loaded flare pistol. The gun was with him all the time but he completely forgot about it. After that incident, the man came to rely fully on God and never took the flare pistol with him when he left the hut.

54. He woke up in a tiny room, the walls of which were white and translucent. He was breathing with ease and, all in all, felt completely happy although the room was a bit too small. "Well, not bad," he thought. After a while, he realized that he was not alone and started to worry. A strange kind of rustle sounded from the other side of the wall. He quieted down but curiosity got the better of him. Faintly, he knocked on the wall. The rustling became louder and someone knocked in response. The unknown behind the wall frightened him somewhat. But the rustle did not seem

dangerous, so he knocked on the wall again. Another response sounded. He started to strike the wall persistently and it began to crack under his blows. The knocking on the other side was also getting louder and it was accompanied by some other sounds, strange and abrupt. Finally, a large piece of the wall fell down and he had to close his eyes tight because of the blinding light that entered. Someone on the other side was helping to break the wall further. He pushed his hand through the hole and, straining his entire body, tumbled out. Strange dazzlingly white creatures with long necks were looking at him with approval making guttural sounds. And suddenly, he grasped the meaning of those sounds, "How sweet he is! How lovely and good!" He felt one of those white creatures, probably the kindest one, caress his back and say, "What a joy! Here is our first baby swan!"

55. A housewife was having a big washing day. She gathered all the laundry in the house and wanted to finish washing it before her husband returned but he came home earlier than usual. Some bed-sheets were already dry and the woman was busy ironing them in another room. The man started to look for some clothes he could change into but could not find anything. "Where is my blue shirt?" he asked. "It's in the laundry!" his wife responded loudly from the other room. "I can't find my white T-shirt!" "In the laundry!" "And the grey trousers are also in the laundry?" the man asked. "Yes, in the laundry!" replied the wife, absorbed by her work. The man went to the kitchen to have a bite, opened the refrigerator and asked, "And where is the cottage cheese and yoghurt?" "Everything is in the laundry!" the wife responded out loud.

56. A newly married couple decided to take a walk downtown. The wife suggested going to a large expensive store. "But for now this is beyond our means, my dear!" the husband said. "Darling, let us just look at the furniture! Maybe one day we will buy something!" The husband conceded and they went into the store. "This dining table would suit us!" the wife said, looking at a beautiful walnut table. "Yes, it would," the husband agreed. "This carpet would look good in our living room," the wife said, pointing at a luxurious carpet. "Yes, it would be fine," the husband nodded. "And this is how we could furnish our bedroom!" "Darling, but that would be too expensive for us!" the husband objected. "But this is so beautiful!" the wife just wouldn't stop. "How obstinate you are, just like your father!" "And you love to throw money around, just like your mother!" the husband responded. "Would you like to

buy something?" the saleswoman addressed them. "No, sorry! We wouldn't like anything!" the newly weds exchanged glances and smiled.

57. Surprised by the long silence in his little son's room, the man looked inside and saw the boy sitting on the floor and enthusiastically taking various screws, wheels and springs out of a mechanical toy. Beside him were other toys, apparently also destined for dismantling. The boy looked up and said, seeing the father's surprise, "Dad, it's interesting to see what is inside all these toys!" "No, no, son," the man said sternly. You should not do that!" "Why, Dad?" the son asked. "Because to make something is much more interesting and useful than to break something. Do you get it?"

58. An old man and his wife lived in a small village. Their little house was aged and they were childless; so, they had to take care of everything themselves. Once it started to rain heavily, the wind moved an iron sheet from its place on the roof and the water began to run into the house through the ceiling. The vexed old man started to walk outside every other minute in order to see when the rain would stop. But the entire sky was covered with clouds and rain continued to pour down. The water kept flowing into the room and the old woman said, "Man, why are you running outside all the time? Don't you see that the water is coming in?" "I see it, that's why I go to look when the rain will stop." "Eh, man! Let the rain fall. The earth needs it. It will not stop faster because of your running. You better go and put a trough in the attic, under the hole so we won't get flooded. And the roof you can repair later when the rain stops!"

59. He who forgets the blooming trees will learn the beauty of spring.
He who forgets the fragrant grass will learn the beauty of summer.
He who forgets the falling leaves will learn the beauty of autumn.
He who forgets the years he has lived will learn the beauty of life.

60. Stony ground is hard to till.
In a dense forest, one does not see the sun.
It is not easy to walk on tall grass.
Because of a multitude of unkind thoughts, it is difficult to live happily.

61. You wash the windows and the room will be light.
You get cured and you will feel your strength renewed.

CONTROLLING THE MIND

You return to your native home and peace will come to your heart.
You free yourself from vain thoughts and you will see the radiance of another life.

62. The bigger a ship is, the less she is tossing.
The bigger a bridge is, the fewer traffic jams are on it.
The bigger a building is, the more austere its design is.
The purer a heart is, the fewer vain thoughts are in it.

63. If you bear a small trouble, you will find a bit of happiness.
If you endure a great misfortune, you will have happiness enough to spare.
Patience with even a little loss is not patience.
True patience has no end.

64. It is uncomfortable to use a rickety workbench.
It is dangerous to ride a jittery horse.
A tree that did not take deep root will fall with the first gust of wind.
A man who doubts is not fit for any work.

65. A beautiful sight:
A seagull soaring over the sea,
A cloud fading away in the sky,
A distant snow-covered summit,
The radiant eyes of an infant.

66. To reproach a person is the same as:
To splatter your eyes with lime,
To cut yourself with a knife,
To swallow melted iron,
To make your life hell.

67. To hold back words of reproach that are on the tip of your tongue is the same as:
To drink some clear water,
To get cured from a serious illness,
To add years to your life,
To be born again.

68. A rotten apple is a bad treat.
A broken watch is not the best present.
A dead man does not stay in the house.
A man with a conceited heart is a living corpse.

69. A traveler was walking down a forest road towards the city. A frightening looking bandit appeared on his way brandishing a dagger and demanded money. The traveler, seeing that the bandit was much stronger than him and well armed, begged for mercy. The bandit paid no heed to the man's pleas, beat him heavily, robbed him of all his money and clothes and went away, leaving the unfortunate victim on the road. The traveler was picked up by another man who was kind looking. He took him to his hut in the forest, dressed his wounds and fed him, but then told the traveler that he would not let him go until his friends paid a ransom. If they would not pay a ransom for him, the traveler would stay with the man forever as a laborer. It turned out that the kind looking man was also a bandit. The traveler pleaded to let him go as his friends had no money for ransom. But the bandit was inexorable. The captive did not know what to do so he decided to escape. Seizing an opportunity, he started running away, while the bandit pursued him. At that time, some guardsmen were going down the road and they saved the fugitive.

70. A man discovered a stone on which there was an inscription, "If you go to the right, you will become a king and will be taken prisoner. If you go to the left, you will become a captive, see many things and escape from captivity. If you go straight ahead, you will gain wisdom." "Well! It is not bad to become a king so let us see!" the man thought and went to the right. He came to a country that had no ruler so the residents of that country elected him king. For a while, he lived in peace, eating and drinking to his heart's content. But then violent nomads attacked his kingdom, burned everything and turned the people along with the king into slaves. "I should have gone to the left!" the man thought and found himself back by the stone. He went to the left and again became a captive of the same nomads. For a long time, he followed them as a slave and saw them attack and plunder various kingdoms. He was languishing in captivity but finally seized an opportunity and escaped. He was now a free man but his health was poor and his strength weakened. It was hard for him to do any work. "Too bad! It seems I should have gone straight ahead!" the man thought and again found himself by the stone. He went straight ahead and saw the road becoming worse and worse. All around, there were precipices, thickets, thorns and

prickles. It was windy, it rained and there was no food. "Here it's a real disaster!" thought the saddened man. "I'd be better off returning to the stone!" So he returned to the stone and went back home.

71. A young man set out in search of happiness. For the journey, his father gave him a signet ring. The father said that he had inherited the ring from his great-grandfather and that it was their family's protection. Three mysterious images were engraved on the seal: a barrel, a herald's trumpet and a maiden's profile. The young man put the signet ring on his finger, received blessings from his mother and father and left his home. He went to the harbor and boarded a ship sailing to far-away lands. The voyage was long. One day, a heavy storm began. The ship sprang a leak and began to sink. The captain and the crew, paying no heed to the passengers, were preparing to abandon the ship. There was not enough room for all in the lifeboats so people started fighting. At that moment, the young man saw a small barrel, grabbed it and jumped into the water. He was carried across the sea for a long time. At last, completely exhausted, he was cast ashore. Here a fisherman's family discovered the young man. Thanks to the affectionate care of those people he recuperated quickly. It is to be noted that the fisherman's daughter looked after him with particular devotion.

After some time, the youth decided to continue his quest. He learned where a city was located and how it could be reached; so, he bid farewell to the fisherman's family and took the road to the city. Soon some armed horsemen caught up with the young man and began to ask who he was and where he was from. They did not believe the young man's story and took him for an enemy spy. So they bound the lad's hands and escorted him to the city. The garrison commander also did not believe the detainee's explanation and ordered to have him taken to the square and executed. The executioner was already preparing to behead the young man when a herald's trumpet sounded. The herald announced to the people that a peace treaty had been concluded with the neighboring kingdom and that the captive would be pardoned and set free.

Overjoyed by this miraculous salvation, the young man hurried to leave the city. On the way, he constantly noticed charred ruins. Soon he encountered some refugees with their miserable belongings. They told the young man that their villages were occupied by rebels who had advanced from the coast and were now fighting against the royal troops. Barely a few hours passed before the young man, along with the refugees, were taken prisoner by angry, armed men. They forced their captives to build ramparts. After some time, drums sounded and the royal troops launched a counter-attack. The soldiers broke through the rebels' defenses killing all of them on the spot without mercy. When they approached the young man, one of the soldiers, also of a young age, recognized him and asked the others not to do him any harm. It turned out that the warrior was in reality the daughter of the fisherman from the coast. Her family had been killed by the rebels but she survived, disguised as a male and joined the royal troops in order to avenge the death of her parents. The young man and the maiden happily embraced each other and decided not to part again.

They found the royal general, kneeled, asked for forgiveness and for permission to get married. The general was much surprised by the incident and sent a messenger to the king. A few days later there arrived a royal decree granting a pardon to the courageous maiden and permitting her to marry the young man. The king also sent them a splendid marriage present. The newly married couple safely reached the young man's native land and settled in the house of his parents. Thus, the barrel, the herald's trumpet and the maiden became the symbols of happiness and wellbeing of that family.

72. A boy asked his father to show him the North Star. In the evening, the father explained to the son how to look for it, showed it in the sky and asked the boy if he had remembered his explanation. "Yes, Dad," the boy replied. After a while, he came to his father again and said that he was unable to find the North Star among other stars. "Son, you should remember that the North Star is always stationary," the father replied, "while other stars move around it. This way, you will always be able to distinguish it."

After taking care of some business, the man went out to the yard and saw his son gazing attentively at the starry sky. "Dad, is that it?" the boy asked, pointing at the star. "Yes, son. And why are you asking?" "Because I am still not quite sure that it is the one." "When you get accustomed to finding the North Star quickly, my boy," the father smiled, "you will never doubt whether it is the one or not."

73. Two friends got lost in the mountains in the summer. Their supply of water quickly ended and they were suffering from thirst. Suddenly the travelers came across the hut of a shepherd who gave them a bucket of clear, cool water. Each of them took a mug, scooped up the water and began to drink. One of the friends was

drinking fast taking big gulps while the other one was sipping the water slowly. The latter asked his friend, "Why are you drinking so fast?" "So that my body gets the water it needs quickly. And why are you sipping?" "I want to prolong the pleasure of drinking good water." They started to discuss which way of drinking water was better. The shepherd heard their argument and said, "Both ways are good. The main thing is to quench the thirst. How is one's own business."

74. It is easy to breathe in a tidy and clean room.
It is easy to walk a road without unneeded burden.
It is easy to be silent when you stop vain chatter.
Ease and joy are felt by a heart that has no unkind thoughts.

75. An unkind thought can come even in a church.
A kind thought can visit even in a prison.
You can be deluded even beside saints.
You can learn the Truth even beside bandits.

76. Two teenagers ran away from home in order to live a free life. Half a day passed, the boys became hungry and remembered their home. "I can imagine how the parents are worried now," one of the teenagers said. "Yes, I feel for them too. What do you think they are doing right now?" said the other. "What do you mean, 'what are they doing'? They are probably having lunch." The boys stayed silent for a while. "I am a little bored without our friends. I wonder what they are doing now?" "What are they doing? They are eating lunch too. What else is there to do?" The teenagers exchanged glances, and one of them suggested, "You know, free life can wait and lunch cannot. Let's run home."

77. A family decided to spend the summer at the country house they had just bought. At first, everyone was trying to get accustomed to the unfamiliar location of the rooms and to the multitude of doors. One night, the electricity was cut off. The husband walked out of the bedroom and went to the kitchen to get a flashlight. After a while, he came back with a flashlight in his hand. He examined everything carefully and left again. He could be heard walking from one room to another, opening and closing the doors. Then his steps sounded loudly and the husband returned to the bedroom again. "What are you looking for, dear?" the wife asked in surprise. "Why

is everything different in our home? I can't understand it in the darkness." "Wake up, honey! We are not at home, we are in the country house!"

78. A man went to see the Nile and liked it very much. When he returned to Russia, he visited his elderly parents who were living in a village near the river Volga. Other villagers came to his parents' house and asked him to tell them about his travels. The man showed everyone his photographs of the Nile, speaking with admiration about the sunrises and sunsets over the river, the beauty of the sailing ships and the fertility of the Nile Delta. Looking at the photographs, the villagers could not quite fathom the difference between the Nile and the Volga. Not knowing how to explain it clearly enough, the man said, "To make a long story short, the Nile is the Volga with crocodiles. "Eh, there you go!" the villagers smiled. "So, the Volga is better!"

79. Tourists in the Caucasus came to a mountain lake surrounded by snow-covered summits. The wind was creating ripples on the lake. "There must be so many fish here," voices said. "These ripples on the surface…must be fish playing." A mountain-dweller who was shepherding his cattle nearby remarked, "If there are any fish here, it must have arms and legs." "Why?" the surprised tourists asked. "Because otherwise it could never climb here," the shepherd laughed.

80. A woman put her six year-old son to bed and went to her room. After a while she returned to see if the boy was sleeping but he was still tossing and turning. "You are not asleep, my dear?" the mother asked. "No," the boy complained. "I close my eyes and try my very best to fall asleep but the more I try, the less it works." "No, dear, you should not do it like that," the woman smiled. "You keep trying to fall asleep and that's why you stay awake. Just sleep. That's it. Okay?"

81. No kind of wind will harm grass, it will just bend lower.
No kind of tempest will stir up the water in the well.
No kind of gale will trouble the depths of the sea.
No kind of circumstances will break a pure heart.

82. The sea casts rubbish ashore.
Dust does not stay in the air for long.
A mean dog will not run in the streets a long time.
The Truth always repels a vainglorious man.

CONTROLLING THE MIND

83. He who keeps his chastity:
Acquires childhood without end,
Inherits youth without disappointments,
Has a great consolation in his mature years,
And by the time of his old age discovers an inexhaustible spring of happiness inside himself.

84. If you don't seek the Truth, then for you:
Your house will become a prison,
Your job will become servitude,
Your friends will become bandits,
Your bad thoughts will become merciless executioners.

85. A nuisance happened to a peasant family: an axe was lost. Everyone was running around looking for it but to no avail. Only the master of the house was not worried. He was just sitting on a bench by the stove. "Father, the axe is lost," his wife, his son and daughter-in-law told him. "It is lost and it will be found," the man replied. "But what are we going to do now without the axe?" they asked him. "We can't even chop wood for the stove." "So, ask the neighbor to lend us an axe." They ran towards the neighbor's. As they were running across the yard, they found the axe by the dog's kennel. A puppy had dragged it away.

86. A family sat down to a dinner and realized that they had no bread left. The father told the son, "Run fast and buy some bread in the bakery before they close." The son took the money and walked quickly. They waited and waited until finally they had to eat what they had. Late in the evening, the boy finally returned home…without the bread. "But what happened, son?" I am sorry! I went outside and the guys told me, 'We are having a game of football and we have no goalkeeper. Help us out.' I thought that it was not right to refuse. Then I got absorbed in the game and forgot about the bread completely. After the game, I remembered and I ran to the bakery right away but it was closed already." "Well, don't do it again," the parents said. The next time they ran out of bread, the father told the daughter, "Please run to the bakery, full speed!" "Yes, Dad," the girl responded. Soon she came back with the bread. "Here, children," the father said. "If you need to do something useful and good, never get distracted by anything."

Mysterious Discourses

87. A man won a large sum of money in a lottery. Not willing to draw attention to himself, he refrained from saying anything to his co-workers although they noticed his happy face. When he was taking a trolley home, the passenger next to him was reading a newspaper that had the lottery results. "Boy, there is a lucky person out there. What a bunch of money he won!" the passenger remarked. The man only nodded, although he felt a terrible urge to say, "It's me. I am that lucky man!" Some old folks who were sitting on the bench outside his apartment building greeted the man and started to tell him that, according to the newspapers, someone in their city had won the lottery. So far, the name of the winner was not known. "Very well," the man said. "It would be great if it were one of our neighbors." When he came home, he shared the joyous news with his wife, asking her to keep the secret as long as possible. But their little son overheard the parents' conversation, ran to the balcony and yelled to his friends in the yard, "Hey, guys, my dad won piles of money in the lottery!"

88. He is living dead:
Who despises a single man,
Who reproaches a single man,
Who judges a single man,
Who hates a single man.

89. One evening, hunters were sitting by the campfire. As usual, they started to talk about this and that. One of them began his story, "When I was young, an amazing thing happened to me. Once, passing through a gorge, I noticed a small opening in a rock. I looked inside and saw a narrow tunnel going deep into the mountain. I climbed inside, lit a pocket flashlight and started to crawl forward. Soon, the tunnel became wider. I was already able to get on my feet and to walk slightly bent over. Then I was even able to stretch to my full height. I don't remember for how long I walked like that but finally I came to a lake. From somewhere above, dim daylight reached the cave. I guess it penetrated through the cracks in the rock. To my great surprise, I saw a small boat on the shore. I got in and started to row across the lake. I don't remember how long I rowed but after some time I saw a small island covered with dense forest. I went ashore and started to walk along a path that led uphill. After awhile, I reached a wooden hut. I knocked and the door opened. I went in and saw two old monks who greeted me with joy and treated me to a modest meal. They told that there were three of them. One had left to take care of some business. When I

CONTROLLING THE MIND

began to take leave..." "May I finish the story for you?" another hunter interrupted the speaker. "Well...you can try," replied the first hunter, surprised. "So when you started to take leave, one of the monks got up and punched you." "What for?" the storyteller asked, amazed. "So that you wouldn't lie!" the second hunter replied.

90. Two friends agreed to meet early in the morning in order to go fishing together. One of them, not seeing his friend at the agreed upon place, called his home. For a while, no one picked up the phone. Finally, the missing friend answered the phone, "Wait a little. I'll just water the flowers and come." Some time passed and the first man called again, "Well, are you coming?" "In a minute. I just want to gather some of my clothes for my wife to wash. Don't worry. I'll be right there." Half an hour later the first man, having lost his patience, made another call, "Are you coming or not!?" "Just a second, it remains only to feed the dog." "Listen," the waiting friend said. "When we arrange to go fishing, it means that you have to put other things aside and come on time. Otherwise, we'll miss the biting time."

91. When the weak endure the strong, it arouses pity.
When the strong endure the weak, it arouses respect.
When one weakens in endurance, it arouses pity.
When one strengthens in endurance, it arouses respect.

92. It was wartime. Fighting begins in the city. One side of the street that led to the church was controlled by the advancing troops and the other side by those on the defense. Violent exchanges of fire were taking place. Nevertheless, an elderly priest used to walk down the street every morning and every evening to celebrate mass. The soldiers kept screaming at him, "Father, do you think you will stay alive? Don't you hear all the shooting?! Stop, don't go there!" And the old man kept responding, "Fellows, I don't think anything! Your business is war and my business is the divine mass. So I'll keep going here like I always did!" Surprised by his words, the soldiers on both sides began to stop shooting when the priest appeared on the street. So he was able to go to the church and return from it safe and sound until the end of the war.

93. When you put trust in your mother, you receive consolation.
When you put trust in your father, you receive wise counsel.

Mysterious Discourses

When you put trust in the Truth, you receive a foundation in life.
When you put trust in yourself, you put trust in your enemy.

94. You rely on your parents. They are not eternal.
You rely on your friends. They are not trustworthy.
You rely on your family. It is not stable.
Only the Truth never abandons man.

95. Dreamers never become men of action.
Men of action are never dreamers.
Those enslaved by their fantasies will never reach the true goal.
And those who seek the true goal cannot have fantasies.

96. If you cling to your youth, you will not be able to keep it.
If you cling to your wellbeing, you will not be able to sustain it.
If you cling to your happiness, you will not be able to safeguard it.
If you cling to the Truth, all the rest will cling to you of its own volition.

97. A group of tourists was walking down a mountain path. Two of the tourists who were in the front saw a bear digging for something in a meadow and came to a standstill, frightened. The rest of the group also stopped. The bear noticed the people, dashed towards the edge of the forest and hid in the bushes. Its unhappy grumbling could be heard from time to time. The tourists who were walking in the rear of the group began to ask, "What's the matter? What happened?" The people in the front replied, "A bear was on our path and it is now in the bushes nearby. Do you hear it grumble?" Mocking voices sounded from the rear, "Are you kidding, a bear? This is thunder, far away somewhere." "If you think that it is thunder," replied those in the front, "You can check who is sitting in those bushes." "No, no," the people in the rear said. "Let us get away from here, fast."

98. Some teenagers from the city came to a village. They decided to take a walk to a forest lake. The locals decided to play a little joke on the city folks and told them, "Be very careful on the forest path." "Why?" the teenagers asked. "Because the bear charges the one who walks first and the lynx jumps from the tree on the one who goes last. "After hearing this warning, the teenagers amused the locals a lot, as they

CONTROLLING THE MIND

started to walk down the forest path in a dense crowd, stumbling and bumping into each other all the time. No one wanted to be the first or the last.

99. It is good to know how to speak well, but not to engage in useless talk.
It is good to know how to think right, but not to ruminate in vain.
It is good to be knowledgeable, but not to be a know-it-all.
It is good to be wise, but not to be pompous.

100. Learn patience, as if you were:
walking a long road,
or climbing a big mountain,
or carrying a heavy burden.

A little,
Then a bit more,
Then a little more...and thus to the very end.

Chapter Five
Mastering Thoughts

If a river erodes the bank, it is reinforced anew.
If a road gets ruined, it is rebuilt every time.
If a garment is torn, it is repaired.
If your attention is distracted, collect it over and over again.

1. A peasant decided to take his son to visit their relatives in Moscow so that the boy could take college entrance exams. The peasant called his relatives and asked them, "What should I bring for you? Some flour?" "No, thank you. We have flour." "Then I shall bring you a sack of potatoes." "Thanks a lot but we have potatoes too." "Maybe some sour cabbage and marinated apples? I would love to bring you some good food, the more the better!" "Please, do not," the concerned relatives said. "Don't bring anything. We have everything in Moscow. Just bring your son and come."

2. A man fashioned a few puppets at home, a bear, a wolf, and a hare and staged a puppet show for his son. The boy loved the show but he could not understand where the hiding place of the two men was who spoke with the voice of the wolf and the hare. The father assured the son that he alone had been speaking for all the puppets, changing his voice. But the boy refused to believe him. "Dad," he said, "I know your voice well and those two other voices I heard for the first time." Then the man pushed away the curtain behind which he was sitting and came out with the puppets. The astonished boy exclaimed, "Dad, you were there alone all the time?! That couldn't be!" "Yes, son, in the theatre anything can be."

3. Two old men were sitting on a park bench talking. "This is no life, these days," one of them said. "When I was young…" The other man nodded in agreement, "Yes, you are right. What kind of life is this? I also remember that when I was young…" But the first old man, who was senior, objected in a feeble voice, "When

you were young, you think that was life? It was over right at that time. The real life, that was when I was young."

4. An old man with a walking stick entered the post office dragging his feet and stumbling. He approached the window where newspapers and magazines were sold. A few people were standing in line. They let the old man go in front of them and the post employee asked him, "Grandpa, what do you need?" And he responded in a trembling voice, "I need the *Health* magazine."

5. Don't stir up the wine before it settles.
Don't stir up the dough before it rises.
Don't stir up the milk before it sours.
Don't stir up the remembrance of God before it takes root in you.

6. When strawberries are on the table, there is no place for preserves.
When fish soup is in the pot, there is no place for canned fish.
When fresh bread is in your hands, there is no place for crackers.
When knowledge is in your heart, there is no place for books.

7. When you have learned the path, you will not be led astray.
When you have comprehended the problem,
   you will make no mistake in the solution.
When you have tested the man, you will not doubt him.
When you have seen the Truth, you will have no more questions.

8. You shouldn't do what is bad for you:
To wear tight shoes,
To buy medicine from street peddlers,
To learn to live from novels,
To search for Truth in human doctrines.

9. It is good to choose the best in life.
It is incomparably better to choose the kindest.
It is still better to choose the wisest.
But the best is to learn to safeguard all these in you.

MASTERING THOUGHTS

10. It is difficult to understand why one needs to endure abuse,
insults,
and scorn.

It is difficult to understand that patience is the ladder to Heaven,
angel's wings,
and reconciliation with God.

11. Don't look for something where there is nothing:
No moon in the pond,
No aid from a scrooge,
No friendship from an arrogant man,
No constancy in this world.

12. A blind man was passing by a factory and ran astray. Lost amidst various industrial buildings, he came to a wide yard. There were no people around. No one to ask for directions. He kept searching and searching for the exit but could not find it. Wherever he went, he ran into a fence. So the blind man had no choice but to go over it. He felt where he could put his foot and started to climb. Fortunately, a watchman saw him and yelled, "Are you blind? Where are you going? There are dogs out there!" And the man replied, "You are right, I am blind. Maybe someone will pity me and show me the way out?" The watchman felt sorry for the blind man, learned where he wanted to go and accompanied him to the road. "There is only one fence in this area and this is the fence by our factory," the watchman said. "How on earth did you get here?" "What do you mean 'one fence'?" the vexed blind man said. "There are fences all over the place!"

13. The cunning of a hunter is in choosing the place for an ambush.
The business of a helmsman is in steering a ship by the compass.
The craft of a mason is in building by the plumb line.
The purpose of a man is in purification of his heart.

14. All those people who:
Went to bed and did not wake up,
Sat down for lunch and did not get up from the table,
Went to work and did not return,

Mysterious Discourses

Desired to be good to someone and had no time...
Did they not all want to live?

15. The world will never be able to give what one looks for in it.
To expect it from the world is the same as:
To cook the book, *On Tasty and Healthy Food*,
To collect candy wrappers, if you like sweets,
To try to find beautiful landscapes on a map,
To search for fidelity and love in people.

16. A very tall man went to buy a coat and took his friends along. He tried on many coats but could not find the right size. Finally, he saw a coat that he liked in the window of one of the shops on the main street. After trying the overcoat on, he said, "This coat is great. Considering how much time I spent looking for something that would fit, this coat is just right." The friends approved, "Yes, this is a good coat indeed. And it suits you. That's exactly what you need." "So you would like to buy this coat?" the salesman asked. "How much does it cost?" the man inquired. When he heard the price he felt very uneasy. "Well, you see...it is a bit too narrow in the shoulders. No...unfortunately, this coat does not fit."

17. On a weekend, two friends decided to go camping in the woods. They overestimated the amount of food they needed to take. They had to go up a steep path to reach a good clearing with a spring. Tired of the long ascent, they sat down under the shade of a tree to rest. One of the friends said, "Okay, the main thing is to drag everything to the top where the path is not as steep; so, it will be easier." And the second man replied, "You know, it has become much easier already." "Why?" the first friend asked. "Because I have left some of my cans in the bush. If anyone needs them, let him take them. I give freely."

18. A man read a wise book and decided to abandon his aged hut, his poor town and his meager salary for the sake of the Truth although he regretted a lot that he had to leave everything behind. He found himself in a big beautiful house surrounded by splendid gardens stretching as far as one could see. In the house, there lived people who, like himself, had abandoned everything in this world. He compared his new life to his past life and it pleased him so much to live well. Some time passed, the man reflected and decided to abandon that life also. Then the entire earth became his

MASTERING THOUGHTS

home, its expanses, his garden and imperishable goods came into his possession. But then the man could not restrain himself. He started to put on airs and to feel proud. At that very moment, he found himself back in his dilapidated house with a meager kitchen garden. At first, the man lamented but then he calmed down and said to himself, "Still, I understood the most important thing. The harm is in pride. I should have abandoned it first of all."

19. It is not easy to carry sand,
It is harder to carry stones,
It is harder still to bear slander,
But the heaviest burden is knowledge in excess.

20. Just as oil never blends with water,
As seagulls and crows never fly together,
As a ray of sun never mingles with darkness,
So you must uphold your way in life.

21. If the prey is too big, the crow lets go of it.
If the burden is too heavy, the donkey lies down on the ground under it.
If the ford is too dangerous, you will not force the horse to step into it.
If the thought is bad and dangerous, never let it enter the heart.

22. In this life, it is good to construct houses,
to plant gardens,
to nurture children.

But it is better to construct your character,
to plant good habits in yourself,
to nurture a good heart.

23. A city dweller got lost in the forest late in the autumn. The first snow had fallen and had drifted over the paths. The man lost his way. He roamed and roamed and finally saw somebody's tracks. The man rejoiced but then he looked closer, he realized that the footprints were his own. So he really lost heart! Where was he to go? Dusk was starting to fall. Suddenly, he heard some dogs barking far away. He went in that direction and reached a village. But then a new trouble occurred. The dogs

ran up to him and he barely escaped being torn to pieces. Fortunately, the locals chased the dogs away. When they brought the city-dweller to his night's lodging, they asked him, "How did you manage to find our village?" "Well, were it not for your dogs, I would never have found you," the man said. "That's true," the locals agreed. "What bites also helps. And our dogs are really vocal. You'll not find the likes of them in the entire countryside."

24. A fellow wanted very much to become a family man. All of his friends had already gotten married. So he took a wife and two children were born to them. By and large, they lived all right, like everyone else. But one day, his spouse left and took the children with her. The man was at a loss. His friends advised him, "Get married again." So he got married. He and his wife lived together for some time then he left her himself. They just could not get along. The fellow met with his friends to talk it over. And they told him, "It is the same with all of us: some divorced, some separated. And those who still live together don't seem particularly happy. That's life for you!" The fellow started to think, "So how should I live? Something is missing here. But what exactly? Hard to tell..."

25. A man lived on the edge of a Siberian village. After living there a long time, he decided to go and look for happiness. He locked the door of his house, propped the gate up with a stick and left. He walked for a long time and around him was Siberian forest without end. At last, he saw the forest getting sparser. "This means there should be people here," the man thought. He walked out of the forest onto a meadow and approached a fence. He walked along the fence and saw a gate propped up by a stick. "But this is my gate and this house is mine. So people are right that the earth is round. Wherever you go, you come back to your own home."

26. A man received his salary, put the money into his coat pocket and headed home. On the way, he met some acquaintances. They talked for a while then took leave of each other. On the way, the man put his hand into the coat pocket and the money was not there. "So it got stolen? But who could do it? Maybe I lost it while I was talking to my friends?" So he ran back, looked on the ground and everywhere, but did not find anything. The man returned home looking as black as thunder. He took off his coat and told his wife, "It seems I lost all the money. Maybe it got stolen." "You made this up, didn't you?" the wife replied. "And where did you put the money?" "In my coat pocket." The wife lowered her hand into the pocket and felt a

hole there. So she stretched her hand further and said, "Here is the money, under the lining!" "You don't say!" the man exclaimed with relief. "And so much went through my mind!"

27. A paleontology expedition came to a distant village in the mountains. The paleontologists met the local residents and a conversation started. "So what are you going to look for?" the villagers asked. "In this area footprints of a cave-man were discovered," the paleontologists explained. "So it's him that we are going to look for." "A cave-man?" asked the surprised villagers. "He never lived here." "That's true," nodded the village elders. "We know every man here but we have never even heard about a cave-man." "He died a long time ago," the scientists explained. "Oh, a long time ago! This means he was probably not from this village."

28. Two geologists were spending the winter at a mountain base. They had little work and a lot of spare time. A heavy snowfall occurred and their house was heaped up with snow. One of the geologists did not know how to occupy himself. "Lie down for a while," advised his colleague who was reading a book. The other geologist lay down but soon got up again. "And what is there to do now?" was his rhetorical question. "Well, keep yourself busy with something," replied the man who was reading. The other geologist began to sort out the rock specimens. In a while, his voice sounded again, "Okay, I am finished with this and then?" "Well, read something," his friend replied. "But I have read all the books we have," the hostage of the elements complained. "Whatever you do here, it is all the same! You can't get away from yourself!" "That's right," his steadfast friend agreed. "And there is actually no need to get away from yourself. Just forget about yourself and you will calm down."

29. First the cow eats hay,
But then it masticates it for a long time.
Knowledge comes fast,
But to master it takes time, often a lot of it.

30. When the fisherman does not put to the sea, there is no fish.
When the artist does not paint, there are no paintings.
When the carpenter does not plane the boards, there are no shavings.
When the heart calms down, bad thoughts stop pestering a man.

Mysterious Discourses

31. A man lived on a busy street in a city. Once, early in the morning, he went to the window as usual. Outside there were cars, crowds, noise and smog. It was not pleasant to look at. "How tired I am of seeing all that," the man thought. "It would be nice if all of it were to vanish," so he thought and went to work.

In the evening, the man came back home. When he was done with his dinner and a few chores, night had already fallen. In the morning, he was struck by unusual quiet. He listened carefully but heard nothing. The man approached the window and saw neither cars nor people. The street was deserted. He got dressed quickly, went outside and saw that he was completely alone. There was no one to ask what had happened. Urban transport was not running because there was no one to drive it. The man managed to reach the office on foot. He tried to find someone, anyone, but to no avail. Exhausted, he returned home and felt that he was scared. "How tired I am of this solitude," the man thought. "It would be nice if everything were to become the way it was before." He listened and heard that cars were already blaring outside. He looked out of the window and again there was noise, smog, a sea of people on the street and the man felt great relief. "It's all right!" he said to himself. "I'll put up with it somehow because to be alone is harder still!"

32. Wolves are bloodthirsty,
Tigers are ferocious,
Bandits are ruthless,
But there is nothing more merciless than bad thoughts.

33. A woman is preparing to go shopping in the city. Her husband, an architect, absorbed by the work that he has taken home, holds out his wallet to her. As she is leaving, the wife asks, "Should I leave some of this money for you, honey?" "The less, the better," responds the husband, drawn to his blueprints. After a while, the woman returns home with big shopping bags and returns the wallet to her husband. The man opens it and says, "But there is nothing in it!" The wife raises her eyebrows. "Of course, there is nothing. I thought that you decided to make a present to me and that's why you said, "The less, the better." "Oh darling, I had something completely different in mind, "The less you spend the better."

34. Once in the summer, three villagers came to the high bank of a river. Underneath, blackthorn bushes were swaying in the wind and the river was flowing smoothly. One

of the villagers exclaimed, "Look, there is a wolf in the bush!" "No, it is too yellow for a wolf," the second villager objected. "It looks like a fox." The third peasant looked attentively and said, "It's moving and you can see white hair. It's probably a hare that has not fully molted yet. Let's move closer." Quietly, trying not to make noise, they walked down a path to the river. They looked and saw a yellow towel with a white pattern left by a tourist on a bush.

35. At an art exhibition, a guide with a group of tourists goes from one painting to another, speaking about the works of modern artists. "Here you can see a bright painting by a young artist. The painting is called 'Morning,'" says the guide, glancing into his catalogue. "Freshness and sincerity of feeling permeates the entire composition. The painting exudes youth and joie de vivre." One of the tourists, after looking at the plate beneath the canvas, tells the guide, "Excuse me, but it appears to be a different artist's work and by a different name. It is called "Evening." "That is strange," says the guide, surprised. "They changed the painting and did not mark it in the catalogue. What a shame. But actually, it does not matter." Glancing in his book again, the guide continues mechanically, "This painting also gladdens us by its expressiveness and optimism. Let us move on."

36. Did you have childhood?
Did you turn seventeen?
Did you turn thirty?
Did you turn fifty?
If yes, then you know very well that all your life so far took less time than is necessary to reply, "I did."

37. A strange glow began to appear and disappear over a village. They learned about it in the city. Scientists came to study the phenomenon. A physicist conducted research and several experiments and concluded, "No, this is not within my field." An astronomer just shrugged his shoulders. They asked the locals how they explained the glow. "It has been glowing like this for a long time. We have gotten used to it," they replied. "But we ourselves don't know what it is." The villagers said that and started to laugh. "And why are you laughing?" asked the scientists, puzzled. An old man came forward, "You learned sirs might not believe it. On that side of the village, the old woman Darya lives. Whenever she starts her prayers, the glow appears. That's the gist of it."

Mysterious Discourses

38. It is dangerous:
When wasps live in your room,
When a scorpion climbs into your clothes,
When a snake settles on your bed.

But it is much more dangerous:
When bad thoughts appear in your heart. Obliterate them immediately.

39. The cat walks up as soon as lunchtime comes.
The dog comes running as soon as it is called.
The cares grow as soon as one remembers them.
The world entangles the soul as soon as one thinks about it.

40. A man came to his friend's country house in the summer. They gave him a room, the window of which faced the yard. At night, the owner's dog was running there. The window was left open because of the heat and the dog, scenting an unfamiliar man, barked constantly. The guest tried to pacify the dog by calling it gentle names but to no avail. Then he found some cookies in the room and fed them to the dog. It quickly consumed the treat and started barking again. Having lost his patience, the guest threw a clothes brush at the dog, then a mug and began searching for something else to throw. At that moment, his friend knocked on the door and asked, "You are not asleep yet?" "Nothing of the kind!" the guest exclaimed. "I am waging war against your dog!" "So let's move you to another room and the dog will calm down by itself," the host suggested. "Very well," replied the guest. "The most important thing is that I'll calm down too."

41. Two friends were travelling in the mountains and found a large cave. Full of curiosity, they switched on their flashlights and went inside. After walking a rather long distance, they saw light, hurried to the exit and came out in a completely unfamiliar place. "Now let us go back," one of the friends suggested "and then we shall understand where this cave leads." They went back, but unexpectedly came out in a new place unknown to them. "Very strange," one of the men said, feeling lost. "At first it seemed clear but now I can't grasp anything." "Then we must return to the way we took first and look carefully where we went astray. Let's go," said the other man. But they again exited not where they had entered the first time. "This is some kind of a mess," the friends resolved and, already starting to despair, walked

into the cave anew. After passing through, they again found themselves in a different place. "No, I can't understand what's happening. This is some kind of a riddle!" exclaimed one of the men. "Yes," his friend agreed. "And I feel too exhausted already to keep looking for the first entrance."

Fortunately, the friends noticed on a meadow near the cave an old man who looked like a mountain dweller. They approached him, described what had happened to them and explained that they were unable to find the place where they had entered the cave the very first time. "So far, no one has managed to find it," the old mountaineer told them. "You will be better off descending to the valley. That way you will get home, albeit in a roundabout way." "And what is the name of that cave?" the friends asked. "Riddle!" responded the old man.

42. A recollection of sour apples makes one frown upon seeing apples.
The words "vegetable garden" make one recall calloused palms.
The tales of past travels make the heart beat faster.
Remembering the world is equal to remembering the vanity of vanities.

43. A man got lost in the woods and came to a hermit's hut. After greeting the old man, the traveler asked, "Tell me, who you are?" "I am you," he heard in reply. "No, that's not the way it goes. I am me and you are you." "Very well," said the hermit. "I am me and you are me." "No, no," the guest objected again. "You should not confuse your 'I' with my 'I.' If you say 'I' about yourself, and I say 'I' about myself," the old man objected, "Then what is the difference between your 'I' and my 'I?'" "What do you mean, what is the difference? I am the guest, and you are the hermit." "And what if both of us are guests?" the hermit asked. "What do you mean?" "You are my guest and I am a guest of this world. So what comes out of it?" "That we are one," the guest whispered in astonishment.

44. School students were having a geography lesson. The schoolmistress asked a student to come to the blackboard. "Please show on the map the highest mountain of Africa and tell us what it is called." The student had not learned the lesson well. He looked at the old map for a long time, then found a mountain with half-erased letters and, poking into it with a pointer, hesitatingly read, "Manjaro." "What, what?" the schoolmistress asked. "Don't get mixed up in words and say it again, please." The student, feeling that the answer was wrong, glanced inquisitively at his fellow

students. One of them whispered, "Kili…" Having heard the prompting, the student replied readily and with confidence, "The highest mountain of Africa is called Manjaro-Kili."

45. A man settled near a mountain next to a spring with wonderful clear water. Once, after descending to the village to buy a few things, he heard a conversation of some local residents about a brook with excellent water that was flowing nearby. The man got very interested and started to ask the villagers how to find that brook. The locals explained that he would have to descend further into the gorge and only in that place would he see the brook flowing from the mountain heights. "And where do you live yourself?" the villagers asked the man. "At the mountain," he replied. "And is there a spring by your house?" "Yes, there is." "What an odd fellow you are! Why do you need our brook if it flows from above, from your spring?"

46. One does not tolerate mice and rats in the house.
One does not breed venomous snakes in a well.
One does not welcome spiders and cobwebs in one's room.
Never let bad thoughts occupy your heart.

47. It is dangerous:
To walk in the forest amidst tall, rotten trees that are about to fall.
To try to stand on crumbling ground.
To cross a river by a broken bridge.

But it is even more dangerous:
To consider this inconstant world reliable.

48. In clean water, there are no dregs.
In a clear sky, there is not a single cloud.
In a clear gaze, there is nothing concealed.
In a pure heart, there is not one bad thought.

49. Endure the pain until the wound heals.
Endure the offence until it passes away.
Do not give up until bad desires vanish.
Do not give up until anger dies.

50. If a river erodes the bank, it is reinforced anew.
If a road gets ruined, it is rebuilt every time.
If a garment is torn, it is repaired.
If your attention is distracted, collect it over and over again.

51. As attentive as the bird may be, the cat is more dexterous.
As careful as the hare may be, the fox is more cunning.
As experienced as the courier may be, he also stumbles.
Do not remain idle even for an instant.
Safeguard your heart more than your own self.

52. A young man was drafted. He missed his home very much and kept counting the days that remained before discharge. The scheduled time approached and the young man and his comrades were already preparing to go home. Unexpectedly, an order came to the unit by which that young man in particular was to be left on active duty for another month because of service needs. The soldier was desperate. He sat down on his bunk, clutched his head and groaned, "I already packed my stuff. I told my family that I was coming and now I have to stay here for a whole month more. I can't take it!" His comrades were trying their best to calm him down. The commander came over and said, for some reason with his mother's voice, "Son, get up! Enough of sleeping!" The young man opened his eyes and remembered that he was already at home for a month and all that was just a dream. "Why did you moan in your sleep, my boy?" his mother said. "I dreamed that I was left in the army for another month and I wished so much to go home. I felt very sad." "Son, your troubles and wishes remain in your dream. Forget everything. You have woken up already," the mother said gently.

53. One rarely encounters:
Dead calm at sea,
Completely clear sky,
A man with a constant and stable character,
A heart without worldly desires and thoughts.

54. To try to drive darkness out of a dark room is a useless fuss that will not enhance the light inside.
But if you throw open the curtains and let a ray of the sun come in,

the dark room will become light and darkness will vanish.
You can never reach the Truth with the aid of a lie.
Nothing bad has a place in the Eternal Good.

55. You want to get honey?
    Don't be afraid of the bees' stings.
You want to admire roses?
    Don't be afraid of their thorns.
You want to be happy?
    Don't be afraid to be kind.
You want to be with the Truth?
    Don't allow bad thoughts.

56. A rotten core deprives the log of its strength.
A single weak thread deprives the rope of its tenacity.
A small lie deprives one of trustworthiness.
The Truth leaves the heart if but a single false thought penetrates it.

57. As the field pushes stones out to the surface,
As the sea casts ashore the dead,
As the camp fire keeps off the wild beasts,
So you must teach your heart to keep off bad thoughts and desires.

58. To speak aloud with those who are not close by is a bad habit.
To speak with them mentally is a dangerous delusion.
To imagine those who are not close by is a bad habit.
To communicate with those images mentally is a dangerous delusion.

59. A man and his son went to the coast. The sun was shining brightly. The afternoon breeze was driving small waves towards the shore. The boy quickly took off his clothes and jumped into the water but the very first wave knocked him off his feet. He rose and tried to battle the waves but he lacked strength and skill; so, the waves kept knocking him down, over and over again. The boy's father saw his attempts from the shore and came to his aid. "Son, you must learn to dive under the waves then they will pass above you and will not knock you down. Look how it is done." And the father dove under a wave. "Now all is clear to me, Dad," the boy said. "But

MASTERING THOUGHTS

I am afraid to dive like this alone. Let us hold hands and jump under the waves together." "No, son. It will not work that way because we shall not be able to move freely. You must learn to dive under the waves yourself. Do it without fear. Let them pass above you instead of struggling with them. Then you will never be afraid of sea waves anymore."

60. A man was living in the mountains. He was drawing water from a spring that was laid round with stones. Dense mountain nettle was growing among the nearby boulders. Once in the summer, the man came to the spring as usual, scooped up some water with a bucket and suddenly noticed a venomous snake sleeping on the stones right by his arm. The snake was awoken by the noise and began to uncoil slowly. The man froze with the bucket in his hands. "My Lord!" flashed through his head. He was within a hair of death.

The snake waited but, not finding the man a threat, slowly retreated towards the nettle brush. Only then did the man catch his breath. The tiniest motion on his part, a leap sideways or even a call for help, would have made the snake charge and bite instantly. Then, he would never have returned home.

61. A flood began in a mountain valley, threatening all the local hamlets. People were being evacuated in a hurry. When the last lorry was about to leave, those who were sitting in the lorry noticed a man by the road. "Stop!" they shouted to the driver. "There is a man left!" "I know him. He does not want to leave. He loves his garden too much," the driver replied. "What garden? He just has three trees," said the surprised evacuees. At a turn they saw another man standing by his house. "Come with us!" they yelled to him from the lorry. "I can't. What will become of my house?" "Forget about the house! It will be washed away anyway," the people tried to convince him. "That's right, no doubt. But it still pains me to leave it," the man waved them off sadly. At the outlet of the valley another man was building a stone barrier around his chicken coop. "Leave it all. Let's go!" the people in the lorry shouted to him. "It pains me to leave the chicken coop!" "And how many hens you have?" "Two hens and a rooster!" "So bring them with you," they offered. The man put his hens in a basket, but, as he was running to the lorry, the hens jumped out and escaped to the bushes, clucking. The owner ran after them. "Don't wait for me!" he shouted to the people. The car, as if saying farewell to the flooded valley, honked for the last time and slowly disappeared behind a bend in the road.

Mysterious Discourses

62. During the war it became necessary to take a defensive position at a distant mountain edge. There existed danger that enemies would try to pass there. A young soldier was ordered to check a path in the area and to set up an observation post. A few hours later the soldier unexpectedly returned and reported that enemy movement had not been observed and that no danger existed. "But you did not fully carry out the order," the commander of the defense group said. "It is not enough just to observe the path and its surroundings. Go back and build the firing defense position. Choose an advantage-ground, dig a trench, fortify it with stones and wait there until morning. If we hear shots in the area, we'll quickly come to your aid. Don't retreat even a step from your position."

63. During the war, male residents of a village were told to go into the woods as the enemy was approaching. Everyone was told not to leave any tracks; so, they could not follow existing paths. It was difficult to walk. One of the villagers was constantly moving here and there to break a branch on a bush. The guide who was also a local asked him why he was doing that. "I am afraid that we shall not find the way home, that's why I am leaving marks," he replied. "Calm down," the guide told him. "Don't break branches. The enemy can use these marks to come after us. The less tracks we leave, the safer our place of refuge will be."

64. Several prominent and wealthy public institutions created, "The Seclusion-Lovers Society." It leased large concert halls to conduct its congresses and conferences. Writers who were members of the society published novels about seclusion. Poets prepared entire verse collections devoted to the subject and composers wrote music on seclusion themes. A play called "Seclusion" was staged. Later, a ballet of the same name was produced based on it. The activities of the society were well received by the public and the society continued to quickly expand its membership. When the next conference was scheduled to take place, the board of trustees mailed exquisitely designed invitations to the participants and made hotel reservations for them. Regular conference speakers were placed by the board of trustees on a special list and made honorary members of the society. But one day from one of those members there came a telegram, "Having taken into consideration the findings of the last conference on the benefits of seclusion, I respectfully apologize for the inability to attend the gatherings of "The Seclusion-Lovers Society" in the future. Presently staying in seclusion, signed former honorary member of the Society, so-and-so."

MASTERING THOUGHTS

65. An apartment in a multistory building caught fire. The flames quickly engulfed the entrance, blocking the tenant's exit to the staircase; so, a man ran to the balcony. The fire engines were already approaching the building. The frightened tenant was waving to the firemen and shouting to them, "Hoist a ladder, fast!" When the fireman at last stretched his hand to the terrified man to help him get over to the ladder, he suddenly began to push his savior away and clutched the railing of the balcony even tighter. The fireman was urging the man to move immediately because the fire was already near and it was getting dangerous to remain on the balcony. But it took the scared man only to look downwards to be seized with fear and shove the fireman away again.

Finally, the firefighter lost his patience and shouted, "Listen, if you don't stop resisting, you will burn to death!" After those words, the man suddenly calmed down and let himself be lowered to the ground. The saved man began to thank the firemen. "Then why were you beating the fellow off?" they asked him. "I don't know myself!" replied the man. "It was scary."

66. Two friends met on the street. "How are you doing?" "Fine, and you?" "Oh, you wouldn't believe it... busy every day. Taking care of this, taking care of that, sometimes I don't even know what to start with. Thoughts are in a whirl." "Maybe you should think a bit less about your business?" the friend suggested. "Are you crazy? Not to think about business? That's impossible!" So they parted. A few days later the friends met again. This time the one who was absorbed by his cares looked even more worried. He kept his hand on his cheek. "What's wrong with you?" the friend asked. "My tooth is killing me; so, I am going to the dentist," he replied. "And what about your business?" "What business? With such a toothache?" "Ah, you see! This means you can forget about your business when your tooth hurts?" "I guess you are right," the suffering man replied and hurried to the clinic.

67. A seven year-old boy woke up very early. The sun had just risen. The birds were chirping merrily. It was summer. What a joy! They called him for breakfast but he did not even notice what was on the table, he yearned so much to run outside to play with the other boys. The breakfast seemed to never end. At last, everyone stood up from the table. The boy ran to the yard to his friends. They played and played and got tired. They rested and began to play again. Then they rested some more. "How much time is left until lunch?" one of the boys asked. "A hundred years!" replied the

smartest of the boys. "So let's go play some more!" the boys shouted. They played so much that everyone's legs were already giving out but lunchtime was still not there. Finally, they heard the parents call everyone for lunch. The boy ran inside, washed his hands, sat down at the table and said, "Mom, and why did it take so long?" "So long? We always have lunch at the same time, at noon," the boy's mother replied. "And I thought that a hundred years passed already. And it's only noon? Great!"

68. Two people are traveling in a car across the desert. As far as one can see, there is neither a single tree, nor a blade of grass. It is blazingly hot and the air over the sand trembles and vacillates. One of the travelers says, "I always thought that in the real desert at least something was growing: thorns, cacti. Here there is nothing at all. Is this real desert? I guess not. There is nothing to look at." "Exactly," his friend agreed. "Elsewhere you can see an oasis where there would be thorns, cacti, even trees. But a real desert is more real the more it is deserted."

69. Spectacles sat upon the man's nose, considered themselves a VIP (very important person) and took on airs. But the comb that sometimes emerged from the jacket pocket considered itself more important than the spectacles. After all, it was admitted to the man's head! And the pen that lay on the table did not dare to think so highly of itself. It was happy just to exist and liked to work. When the man took it into his hand, it was always anxious not to make a mistake. After all, the man entrusted his thoughts to it. So the pen always tried to rise to the occasion. Only the paper was completely indifferent - write whatever you want. For the indifference, it had to endure the most of all. The man frequently crumpled it, tore it to pieces and threw it into the basket. As for the pen, the man always took it with him when he was traveling and tried not to part with it and the pen was very grateful for that.

70. A man went to a doctor's appointment. "I am ill, doc," he complained. "I tried all kinds of medicine and nothing worked. I am already losing faith in doctors." "Please let me examine you," the doctor suggested. After the examination, the doctor said, "All in all, there is nothing terrible. But still it would be better to go through some tests in order to determine why exactly you are not feeling well. Then we shall be able to offer you the necessary treatment." "Oh, there is so much trouble with those tests," the patient said with a downcast air. "Besides, I seriously doubt that any of it will help me." "Indeed? In this case I also tend to doubt that you will ever feel better with such an attitude towards your treatment," the doctor said.

MASTERING THOUGHTS

71. A calf was tied to a peg in a meadow. It tired of going around with a rope on its neck; so, it tried to break loose. The calf kicked and panted without any result. It looked up and saw a lorry carrying cows. The calf felt so sad. It wanted so much to run after them, to ask them to take it along, that its eyes filled with tears. The calf lowered its head and stood still in sadness. Then it overheard its master speaking to a neighbor, "They took the cows to the slaughterhouse, did you see?" "I did. And what are you going to do with your calf?" "My heifer, you mean? Let it live. A good cow always comes in useful."

72. Honey is pumped from combs into a honey-press.
Grains are ground into flour at a mill.
Coal is extracted from a bed in a mine.
The Truth can only be found in the heart.

73. You can entrust your life only to someone:
Who will never change,
Who will never let you down,
Who will never forsake you,
Who will always help.

74. The good is neither inside nor outside,
It has neither ignorance nor a lot of learning.
Happiness comes, but it has no legs.
Love supports all, but it has no arms.

75. The closer to the sea, the fresher the air is.
The closer to the hives, the stronger the aroma of honey is.
The closer to the city, the brighter the lights are.
The closer to the Truth, the more miracles you see.

76. If you make a sharp jerk to lift even a feather, you may get a sprain.
If you break even a straw, you may injure yourself.
If you are nervous, you can get upset even when eating sweets.
If you are angry, even giving alms will do no good.

Mysterious Discourses

77. If you were to know that you would stay alive only as long as a candle is burning,
   what kind of candle would you light?
If you were to know that your next breath would be the last,
   what kind of breath would you take?
Just as your past slipped by, so your present will fly by.
To try to hold your life here, is the same as to try to hold smoke in your hand.

78. It is not easy to find:
The one who is always on time, but never hurries.
The one who does everything, but no one sees it.
The one who knows everything, but no one realizes it.
The one who helps everyone, but tells no one about it.

79. Have you ever been woken up at night by claps of thunder in the spring?
Have you ever been woken up by the first rays of sun entering your room?
Have you ever been woken up because happiness was overflowing your entire heart?
If yes, all of that bears just a faint resemblance to what you feel when Life opens up
   in you.

80. When there are no mosquitoes, the summer evening is even more beautiful.
When there is no city noise, the spring morning is even more splendid.
When there is no anger in the heart, patience turns into joy.
When there is no envy in the heart, all people appear as angels.

81. A young man had to urgently deliver some medicine to herdsmen high up in the mountains. He woke up early in the morning. Dark clouds were visible over the summits and thunder roared threateningly. Doubt began to penetrate the young man's heart. He thought, "Maybe I should not go today?" But then he forced himself to get ready, took a raincoat just to be sure and set out with resolution. It began to drizzle. But the higher the sun was rising from behind the mountains, the lighter the sky was becoming. When the young man climbed high enough, already he saw the sun disperse the last clouds. The sky became completely clear. He reached the herdsmen and handed them the eagerly awaited medicine. The young man told the herdsmen that in the morning he had been hesitant to go up into the mountains because of the danger of a thunderstorm. The herdsmen just smiled, "The morning clouds, even if they do look threatening, do not always bring a storm. Usually by

noon they disappear completely. So no elements are a threat to the one who goes forward bravely!" "Just like in life," the young man thought. "This is a good lesson for me. If you bravely confront danger, it retreats and vanishes by itself."

82. A villager who was a jack-of-all-trades heard that the king was very kind and was rewarding with an open hand any man bringing him a gift. So he carved a very beautiful casket for the king and decided to go to the palace with it. But he decided that, in case the rumor about the king's generosity was not true, it would make sense at least to sell some souvenirs in the city. Putting them in a sack, the man took the casket and went to the palace gates with it. The guards asked the man why he wanted to see the king. "I would like to give His Majesty a present of this casket that I have carved with my own hands." "Very well," said the guards. "Come in." The villager lifted his sack but, as soon as he stepped forward, the guards blocked his way with their spears. "You cannot go to the czar with a sack." The man began to plead with the guards but they were inflexible. "But what am I to do with the sack?" he asked. "Leave it here," they replied. "Oh, how it pains me to leave it! Something will get stolen," the peasant said to himself. "So I will suffer losses or maybe my entire sack will disappear and the king will not reward me with anything. But, on the other hand, when shall I have a chance to see the king again?" So he decisively put down his sack, took only the casket and was led into the palace. The casket was truly pleasant to look at and the king liked it very much. He ordered it to be filled with gold coins and to give all that gold to the villager. Happy, he went out of the palace. "Hey, take your sack!" the guards called to him. "Take all that is in it. It's yours!" the villager replied. "After the king's reward, I have no use for it."

83. Three travelers heard a wondrous old legend about a Heavenly City that sometimes descends to the earth. They wanted to see the city and went in search of it. After long wandering, the travelers saw the great Beautiful City encircled with high walls. They went around it but failed to find a gate or any other entrance. Only in one place, they noticed an odd round opening in the wall through which one could glance inside. The first traveler looked in the opening and silently fell down by the wall. "This is strange," the second traveler said. "What could he possibly see there?" Then he also looked in the opening but, just as his comrade before, fell down wordless. The third traveler, afraid to gaze in the opening, ran over to his comrades who were stretched on the ground. He wanted to ask them what they saw, but they were lying like the dead. Engulfed with curiosity, he approached the opening with great care and

tried to look inside. But at that very moment, without making a sound, he also fell on the ground next to his companions.

They did not remember for how long they lay like that. Regaining their senses, the travelers realized that they were blind and unable to speak. They only exchanged handshakes to cheer each other up in some way. Gradually, speech returned to them but they were still without vision. Slowly, groping their way, they went by a road in order to find some habitation because the Heavenly City had disappeared. A merchant caravan picked them up and took them to a night lodging. There the travelers began to ask each other what they had seen in the opening of the wall of the Heavenly City. The first man said that he had seen something like a bolt of lightning. The second man said that he had been blinded by bright rays that had emerged from the opening. And the third man said that he had not had a chance to see anything because he had lost consciousness as soon as he had brought his face near the opening. In the course of time, the travelers regained their eyesight but they were still unable to tell anyone what exactly they had seen or where one could find the mysterious Beautiful City, encircled with walls without gates - the City in which the wondrous Light lives. They only knew for sure that the Light of the Heavenly City was printed upon their hearts and that one day they would certainly become its citizens.

84. A long time ago a man was lost in the woods and met a giant who caught the traveler and told him in a thunderous voice, "From now on you shall be my slave!" But the man found courage enough to reply, "No. You better kill me, but I will not be your slave!" The giant roared in anger and struck the captive. The man fell down but, when he came back to his senses, he said to himself, "I'll endure the beating but I'll not surrender to him!" He looked at the giant and was very surprised because his tormentor became less tall. "Either you become my slave or I'll kill you!" the diminished giant shouted ferociously. And new blows showered upon the man. But with each blow, the giant was getting shorter and shorter. Soon, he turned into an ugly dwarf. Then the man rose to his feet, staggering and paying no heed to the pain from the blows, laughed, "Here you are! You cannot bear man's patience. That's why you lost your strength and height. Now, I don't fear you!" Having heard these words, the dwarf trembled all over, shrank and disappeared into a crack like a mouse. From that time on, he never appeared to man who had triumphed over him through fortitude and patience.

MASTERING THOUGHTS

85. If you don't guard the orchard, birds will pick away all the cherries.
If you don't struggle against the rats, the house will fall down.
If you don't stop ill feelings, they will develop into hate.
If you don't safeguard the heart, bad thoughts will bring it to ruin.

86. There lived a very gifted preacher who knew how to speak well but was noted for being irritable and hot-tempered. As time went by, he came to realize that his sermons had actually converted few people to moral life. "It would be better if I pay attention to myself, to my drawbacks and try to follow what I preach," the man thought. From that point on, he no longer spoke at length and his renown for being an eloquent speaker gradually faded. But, to the preacher's great joy, more and more of the people he knew began to follow his example in struggling against bad habits and eradicating them. Once the preacher asked a person he trusted, "I wonder why so few people followed my beautiful sermons about moral life. And now, when I hardly give any sermons, so many began to change their lives." The preacher's friend replied, "You see, when you stopped speaking, the Truth began to speak instead of you. And when you were preaching, the Truth was silent."

87. Some calculate their profit and others try to forget about it.
Some try to gain as much as possible and others to lose as much as possible.
On one shore they weep because they have not enough fun and on the other shore they like to weep.
On the one shore they pity those who like to weep and on the other shore they pity those who weep because they have not enough fun.

88. Once there existed the Old Kingdom in which the lifespan of the people was constantly shortening and came to be very short. Its residents heard that the new king had founded the New Kingdom in which people would be able to live forever. Many began to go in search of that New Kingdom. One young man also went. At first, he followed a road where there were many fellow travelers. Soon he began to meet people going back. They were asking those people, "Why are you returning?" And they were replying, "When you reach the end of this road, you will see everything for yourself." Finally, the young man reached a place where the wide road ended and a multitude of narrow paths went in different directions. Some people were standing

there in confusion, not knowing which path to take. Others were going forward but were soon coming back. And some left and did not return.

The young man stepped on a path that appealed to him and set off. Soon he saw warriors blocking the way with their spears and asked them, "What is ahead?" The warriors replied, "Ahead is the Way of Repentance." "And where is the New Kingdom?" "Beyond Repentance." "And how can one enter the New Kingdom?" the man continued to ask. "He who wants to pass from the Old Kingdom to the New must die in repentance. Only then, will he be able to be born in the New Kingdom," the warriors explained. "And will all be born in the New Kingdom when they die?" "We do not know that. This is known only to the king himself." The man thought deeply, not knowing what to choose. Then he decided to ask another question, "And why are there so many paths around?" "People want to bypass us, hoping to enter the New Kingdom without the Way of Repentance," the warriors replied. "But that is impossible because all paths lead to our outpost".

The man stood still some more then he went to check if the warriors were telling the Truth. Indeed, whichever path he took, it led to the Outpost of Repentance. What was he to do? To go back meant to see his life end soon and to go forward meant to die in Repentance.

So he decided that it was better to die on the Way of Repentance for the sake of the New Kingdom. The Old Kingdom was known to him and he did not feel like returning there at all. Ahead there existed the possibility to be born in the new king's endless life. The man stepped forward with resolution and the warriors parted and deferentially let him enter...

A little boy was running across a green dewy meadow and he was full of joy. He knew that he would never die as the Eternal Sun of the New Eternal Kingdom was shining ahead.

89. In great antiquity, next to a city on a mountain, there stood a Dismal Castle and in the castle there lived a wicked sorcerer. He imposed heavy taxes on the city dwellers and subjected them to various calamities. But no one dared to fight against him because the power of his sorcery was great. When the people's suffering became completely unbearable, they held a council to decide what to do. One elder remembered a legend about the pure heart of a youth that would be impervious to

the sorcerer's magic charms. But who among the young men could say that his heart was pure? All of them refused to fight with the wicked sorcerer. At that time, a beautiful white dove flew over a taciturn young man standing aside and the people's unanimous choice fell on him. Those gathered began to tearfully implore the young man to come to their aid and battle against the wizard. "Your tears torment my heart," the chosen one said quietly. "I shall try to carry out what you are asking me." They brought him a sword and armor and the young warrior went towards the Dismal Castle.

The ravens, after noticing the young man on the deserted road, began to croak, so the sorcerer surmised that the people had elected a warrior to fight against him - a mighty sorcerer! He laughed viciously and shot his charmed arrows at the man. At the same moment, the youth felt that he was riding an unbridled stallion dashing madly towards a precipice into which he would fall down together with the horse. Exerting himself, the young warrior recalled the unfortunate people of the city and compassion towards them destroyed all the wicked charms. Everything vanished and he found himself in front of the castle.

The sorcerer retreated from the first chamber to the second, after losing a third of his powers. He shot at the man even more powerful and terrible magic arrows that turned into a great army. Swords glared and spears flew. The enemy soldiers surrounded the daring man. The youth was fighting them off with all his might. Blood was already running from his shoulder and the enemy commander raised his spear to pierce his chest but the young warrior collected his last bit of strength and remembered the defenseless citizens. Courage revived him. He charged the enemy and at that very moment, the charms were destroyed and the army vanished.

The infuriated sorcerer retreated to the third chamber of the castle, after losing another third of his powers. He shot at the young man all of the burning arrows that remained. Flying out of the castle, the arrows turned into a charming young woman. She smiled at the young man bewitchingly and said, "You have won, oh courageous and handsome warrior! The wicked sorcerer escaped from the castle. I was his captive, and you saved me. Taste the refreshing nectar that I have prepared for you and then I shall dress your wounds." She held forth a cup with a beverage to which deadly poison had been added. Charmed by the courtesy of the young beautiful woman, the warrior lost caution, took the cup with poison and raised it to his lips. At that moment, a white dove fell from the sky like a stone and knocked the deadly cup out of his hands. But a few drops touched the dove and it fell dead before the young man's eyes. The warrior came to his senses, surmised the sorcerer's design and loudly exclaimed, "Wicked sorcerer, you will not escape my just revenge!" At that moment the young woman disappeared and the warrior saw in front of him the sorcerer himself. He charged the young man, trying to terrorize him with a sword but the young man fended off the thrust, knocked the sorcerer off his feet and bound him tightly with a rope. At that instant, the Dismal Castle turned into a black cloud that whirled and dispersed into the air.

The happy residents of the saved city sent the sorcerer to the king who put him in a dungeon. And for the young man, the king ordered to cast a shield with a coat of arms depicting a white dove soaring over a golden heart. The inscription on the coat of arms read: "A pure heart is invincible."

90. To see the beauty in life means to already have it in you.
To see the good in life means to already acquire goodness inside.
To see the wise in life means to already possess wisdom.
To see the pure in life means to already attain purity in your heart.

91. What can you sacrifice your life for?
For your mother's and father's salvation,
For your loved ones' salvation,
For your own salvation,
For the love of Truth.

92. You will recognize your mother and father even in a big crowd.
You will choose a favorite book among a thousand other books.
Happiness can be recognized even in the darkness of the night.
Once you learn the Truth, you will not confuse it with what resembles the Truth.

93. He who lifts weights becomes stronger.
He who tries to remember more becomes brighter.
He who cleanses himself of evil becomes kinder.
He who holds by the Truth becomes simpler every day.

MASTERING THOUGHTS

94. If something does not go right in your life,
    hold onto humility and you will not go wrong.
If danger threatens you, hold onto humility and danger will disappear.
If you find yourself in a blind alley, hold onto humility and an exit will be discovered.
Even if chasms yawn before you, hold onto humility and you will be saved.

95. It is good that there exists the unchanging,
the eternally free,
the unblemished.

It is good that it is impossible to change it,
to subjugate it,
to blemish it.

96. You go forward, it meets you there.
You go backwards, it awaits you there.
You look up, it protects you.
You look in yourself, it observes you.

97. One acquires, the other just desires.
One carries out, the other just guides.
One responds, the other just has insight.
One creates, the other just suffers.

98. A group of students went camping in the mountains and got lost in the forest. Trying to find the way, they came upon the hut of a hermit. He was a gray-haired man in shabby clothes. He greeted the lost students with courtesy, offered them tea and crackers and explained how they were to find the path. The young people, embarrassed at first by this unexpected encounter, started to feel more at ease and asked the hermit for permission to put a few questions to him. He consented. "Could you tell us, would you not like to become a renowned engineer, for example?" "No," the hermit replied. "And would you not like to become a great scientist?" "No, I would not." "Maybe the president?" the students joked. "Not at all." "And still, what would you like to become?" "What I am," the hermit responded. "Why? Can you explain it?" the young people asked. "Because even an instant of this life is incomparable to the entire life of any man, whatever his profession is."

Mysterious Discourses

99. A family moved to a new apartment. At first, they were quite content but then an unpleasant peculiarity of the new lodging became known. The neighbor above was a woodcarving enthusiast. He brought tree stumps to his apartment and made various handcrafts out of them, using a hammer and a chisel. The family endured the constant knocking from above for a while but then they lost patience and asked the neighbor at least not to make noise during the night. "I am awfully sorry," the neighbor responded with dignity. "In the daytime, I am at work and at night inspiration comes to me. Woodcarving is an art." So the family from below heard the answer and went away having achieved nothing. About a month later, the knocking in the neighbor's apartment stopped and unusual quiet set in. The neighbors from below met the amateur woodcarver in the yard and asked him what had caused the lull. "The reason is that I have become interested in painting. This is a lofty art!" "Absolutely! We congratulate you!" the neighbors rejoiced sincerely. "Painting is a very lofty and, what is essential, a quiet art."

100. The apparent is not true.
The not apparent is true.
What is alive does not live.
What is not alive never dies.

Chapter Six
Silence of the Heart

The further away you are from home, the harder it is to return.
The more often you look at the clock, the slower time drags.
The more you long for the sunrise, the longer it does not come.
The more you are distracted, the harder it is to return to the heart.

1. He who enters the house does not use an umbrella.
He who dives into the sea does not take clothes with him.
He who falls asleep does not reply.
He who has just been born does not speak.

2. If you don't use the path, it becomes overgrown.
If you don't add wood to the campfire, it dies out.
If you don't live in the house, it comes to ruin.
If you don't recall the world, it forgets about you.

3. A royal tax collector was always sitting by a pillar at the market square. Once, a man who was passing by lost a wallet with money in it. The tax collector quickly rose from his place, grabbed the wallet and hid it in his clothes. But one of the merchants, whose shop was right across from the pillar, saw what happened. He found the man who had lost his money and had already realized that his wallet was missing and was in grief. Together they went to the tax collector and asked him to return the money. The collector began to say that he knew nothing and had not taken any wallet. A crowd gathered. Some people were on the tax collector's side, others tended to believe the merchant. The tax collector kept stubbornly denying everything and finally got vexed and exclaimed, "If what this man is saying is true, then it is also true that this pillar can speak!" To everyone's amazement, the pillar pronounced, "True!" From that time on, no tax collector wanted to sit by the pillar that people named, "The Truthful."

Mysterious Discourses

4. When the moon hides in the clouds, silence becomes more audible.
When the stove is not stoked, the cold is felt more intensely.
When clouds disappear, the sky becomes boundless.
When cares disappear, the heart becomes limitless.

5. If you find a prudent man, live by his side and you will truly live.
If you don't meet such a man, live in humility and you will truly live.
If you acquire purity of heart, live with it and you will truly live.
If you don't acquire it, live in humility and you will truly live.

6. In the spring, a retired professor of science was sitting on a bench in a city park. A little brook was running along the path. Suddenly the professor noticed a toy ship made of paper drifting with the current. The scientist stretched his weak senile hand and took the little ship made out of a magazine page. He carefully unrolled the paper and, noticing an article with a brief description of cosmological theories, began reading. Some scientists believed in the existence of a multitude of worlds parallel to our world. Others thought that our world and the other worlds existed on different levels or in different dimensions. And a third school supposed that somewhere in the universe there were already highly developed worlds capable of helping the earthlings to solve their problems and it was necessary only to wait patiently for the time when they revealed themselves. After finishing reading, the professor just smiled, folded the page back into the toy ship and lowered it into the brook. Rolling gently, the ship unhurriedly sailed on.

7. A young man from a mountain village heard the elders say that in bygone times a few people had been able to see a beautiful and strange flower blooming in the forest and vanishing at once. They said that the one who saw the flower would never forget its unusual beauty. Some people believed that story. Others just laughed. Once the young man was crossing a mountain pass in the summer and stopped to spend the night in an empty shepherd's hut in a meadow. In the middle of the night, he suddenly awoke and saw a faint glow that was diffused everywhere. He came out of the hut. The light was flowing from a nearby dell. The young man ran there and saw something akin to a plant rising swiftly out of the ground but it was not a plant because it consisted entirely of light. Its top was iridescent and emitted a marvelous shine. However closely the young man looked, trying to understand what was in front of him, he failed to discern any distinct outline. He just saw the glow. When he

stretched out his hand, the glow diminished and dispersed into the air with the first faint waft of wind. When the young man returned home and told what he had seen, people asked him to describe what the flower of light looked like but he only shrugged his shoulders and kept saying, "I did see the flower but I cannot tell you what it was like. I don't know the right words to explain how beautiful it was." People were only shaking their heads, thinking that at night in the mountains one is easily deluded. Only one old man took the young man aside and told him in a very low voice, "Son, I have also seen that flower. But don't tell everyone about it, so that you don't become a laughingstock of the people. You should speak about the magic flower only to those who believe you."

8. A young disciple of an elder was forced to return to the world in order to help his parents get out of a predicament. The elder did not desire that but the disciple persisted and left for the city. Family affairs delayed the disciple for a long time. He had to earn money; so, he became a merchant and still was having difficulties making ends meet. A year later, another disciple of the elder found the young man in the city. "What word did the elder pass along?" the young man asked. "The elder wanted me to convey to you that you must stop the whirlpool. Then you will acquire that which is priceless." "But there is no river in our city. Where would one find a whirlpool here?" the puzzled young man asked. The second disciple only shrugged his shoulders with sympathy and left.

Soon, the young man went to another city on business. He sold his merchandise with difficulty and was hardly able to cover his expenses. The young man was staying at an inn that was located near a small but rapid river, on the banks of which one could see some dried-up irrigation channels and a long inoperative dam. It was hot so the young man decided to go for a swim. But the innkeeper warned the young man that the current was quite strong and downstream from the inactive dam there was a very dangerous whirlpool. "For a long time, people have been unable to repair the dam to irrigate their fields. Once, enemies fell upon our country and the elders of the city ordered the workmen to open the dam. Water stopped reaching the fields and this whirlpool formed," he explained. "And what happened then?" asked the young man, moved. "Many brave men perished in the whirlpool, including my own son. They were trying to stop that whirlpool." "But for what purpose?" the young man asked. "On the bank there is a stone with a mysterious inscription. No one knows what it means. But they say that it relates to the whirlpool and how to great riches."

Mysterious Discourses

The young man remembered his elder's words and went towards the river. The water drawn in by the whirlpool was raging and boiling. Next to the dam, the young man saw the stone that the innkeeper had told him about with the carved inscription, "Leap and you shall find." "This is strange. Why would one need to leap into the whirlpool if so many people have already perished in it? Something is wrong here," the disciple reflected, peering attentively at the inscription. Suddenly, its sense was revealed to him. The young man called the innkeeper and some laborers. Together, they moved aside the heavy stone and it turned out that it was covering an opening in the rock, akin to a shallow well. The young man took a torch, leapt in and saw an underground passage that led him to a small cave. There, he saw a stone slab that was the dam's outlet sluice. It was placed in a stone chute upon copper rollers and beside it lay a sledgehammer. With the sledgehammer, the disciple knocked out a copper wedge holding the sluice in place, so that it started to slide along the chute and locked the dam's gate.

The bottom of the gorge, downstream from the dam, began to get dry. Water started to fill the irrigation channels and the happy event grew jubilant crowds. The innkeeper and the workers were joyous to see the young man emerge from the well. Meanwhile, as the water level fell, a grotto in a shoreline rock became exposed. Inside, there was a wrought iron chest. In front of the people, the smiths opened it and saw that in the chest the city treasure lay hidden from the enemies. The people lavishly rewarded the young man and entreated him to stay. But the young man said that it was not he who had helped them but his elder who had ordered him to stop the whirlpool. The young man gave his heartfelt thanks to the citizens, "Here I have found your love and recognition and I am very grateful for that. But here I have also acquired something else, the most important thing for me: the realization that it is time to stop the whirlpool of my attachment to life. That's what is priceless." The disciple left part of the money to his parents, gave the rest to the poor and left the world forever, returning to his elder.

9. When they add lime to mortar, it becomes strong.
When they put red-hot iron into water, it becomes durable.
When man endures suffering, he becomes patient.
When the heart submerges in Truth, it becomes steadfast.

10. If you don't wander into a ravine, you will not flush the crows.
If you don't walk through a slum, you will not run into robbers.
If you are not allured by a passion, you will not fall into an attachment.
If you don't allow a thought about the vain world, you will not be entrapped.

11. Don't blame the rain if the roof is leaking.
Don't blame the puddles if the shoes are torn.
Don't blame the cat if the larder is open.
Don't blame others if you are guilty yourself.

12. Mercury repulses stone, but dissolves gold.
A sieve sifts flour, but does not let straw through.
An orchestra conductor does not tolerate the least false note.
Don't allow a single bad thought into the heart, hold only to the good.

13. Leaving an orchard, we take away with us not the trees but the fruit.
Leaving life, we take away with us not the body but the deeds.

14. When sheep assemble, they crush snakes with their hooves.
When swallows gather into a flock, they chase away the hawk.
When elk form a tight circle, they drive away wolves.
The heart, having collected its strength in prayer, drives away every kind of evil.

15. A rich man is complaining to his acquaintances, "I am not doing well at all. I am almost a pauper." "And what happened?" "What do you mean 'what'? Ivanov has three million, Petrov has five million and Sidorov has ten million." "And you?" "I only have one million left. What shall I do? I am at a loss." "But why are you counting other people's money? Count your own." "But it is I who lent it to them!"

16. A village youngster did not want to work his field and hired out as a goat shepherd. He thought it would be pleasant to spend all day outside at his ease and breathe fresh air. But the work turned out to be very taxing: now the goats would wander into thorny bushes, now they would climb the rocks, now they would help themselves to someone's kitchen garden. In the latter case, the young herdsman would hear a lot of things from the angry villagers. The lad grew thin, the goats exhausted him and he no longer had nature and fresh air on his mind. His friend

pitied the lad and advised him, "Try to shepherd cows. They are calmer." So the lad began to shepherd cows and with them, new troubles appeared. Cows are stubborn and disobedient. The young herdsman kept running after the cows and the cows kept running into the forest. And the cows' owners were complaining, "Where is the milk?" The lad's friend met him again and asked, "So, how is work?" "As bad as it can be," the vexed shepherd replied. "It seems to me that it is not my kind of work at all." "Well, if it is not your kind, why don't you take care of your field?" The lad went to his field and began to weed it and throw out the stones. He saw that it was also not easy. "It is all right," he consoled himself, "At least I am free! No goats, no cows. And as much fresh air as I want."

17. Two booklovers met and stopped to talk. "What is new?" the first man asked. "I got a good book. I liked it a lot," the other said. "And what was it about?" "About life in general." "I would like to read it, bring it over." A few days later, on the weekend, the owner of the book came to his friend's place. He found the friend busy with his dog. He was teaching it to return a stick to him. "Oh, hello! See, I bought a dog. I am training it every day," the friend said. "And I brought you the book, like I promised," the guest replied. But the happy dog owner was already so carried away by the training process that he was no longer listening to his friend. "Why don't you leave the dog alone?!" the guest exclaimed. "Here is the new book, look at it!" "Oh, the book..." the dog owner turned around. "And do you have anything about dogs?"

18. A tiger tamer must be brave.
A horse breaker must be dexterous.
A snake catcher must be courageous.
He who tames impurities in one's mind must be fearless.

19. A young man is preparing for college entrance exams at home. His friends keep coming over and distracting him. "Let's go to the river!" they shout from the yard. "I am coming!" the youngster yells back, closes his books and leaves. "Let's go to the forest!" his friends shout the next day. "Okay!" the young man replies and moves away the books again. "Let's go play volleyball!" they yell the next day. "Just a second!" he replies and gets up from the table. The youngster's father sees that his son is not studying enough and tells him, "Son, I advise you not to waste your time. Read more!" "I shall try, Dad, but it is difficult to refuse friends." "Be your own

master. This way you will help both yourself and your friends. And the earlier you understand my words, the better."

20. He who knows how to wade mountain rivers is not afraid of fording them.
He who knows how to make a campfire quickly is not afraid of rain in the woods.
He who knows mountain passes does not fear the mountains.
He who knows the Truth does not fear any obstacles.

21. An art collector bought a painting by an unknown artist and placed it in his home. Some friends learned about his purchase and asked for permission to come and look at it. "You are welcome! Come any day, any time," the collector assured them courteously. But whenever they would come, the host was not at home: now he would be already gone, now he would not be there yet, now he would have an important business meeting. His friends were very unhappy. Finally, they came to the collector's office and told him, "You know, we are ready to come on a day you choose! Just please be at home at the appointed time! We ask for nothing else!"

22. Once a lover of distant voyages was unable to go anywhere on vacation. So he stocked up on maps, guides and atlases and began to make up various exciting travel routes. He became interested in Africa, followed the equator for some time, then reached the Sahara, crossed the Mediterranean and got stuck in Italy. There was just too much he wanted to learn. The man's wife walked into his room to see what her husband was occupied with. "What are you doing with all these maps?" she asked. "Oh, you see, I crossed from Africa to Italy and got stuck there. So many places of interest! And so little time - only two weeks. I've got to get home in time," the man replied preoccupied. "Darling, are you not home?" the wife asked, puzzled. The husband with difficulty turned himself away from the map, looked around and said, "You don't say so! I am really home! And I thought I was in Italy."

23. They receive guests in one room and live in another.
Outside, the suit is on the man and at home it is in the closet on a hanger.
What is interesting in one city does not arouse interest in another.
What is necessary in one country is quite useless in another.

24. The further away you are from home, the harder it is to return.
The more often you look at the clock, the slower time drags.

Mysterious Discourses

The more you long for the sunrise, the longer it does not come.
The more you are distracted, the harder it is to return to the heart.

25. Two men from the church community began discussing, "Where could we learn about salvation?" They looked at the posters, "See how many lectures there are for the Orthodox. For example, on the "Collapse and then the Apocalypse: Are we under attack?" They went and listened. It was not quite what they were looking for. Maybe it would be better to attend the lecture, "On the church calendar?" They went and listened but did not hear much said about salvation. The men looked at the posters again, "On marriage and family." They went to that lecture and said to each other, "No, this also is not what we are looking for at all." The two men went outside and began discussing again. It occurred to them to ask one of the faithful for advice. They saw an old man walking by, "Grandpa, are you a believer?" "I am." "Can you tell us how one can be saved?" "Saved?" the old man repeated. "You don't know?" "No, we don't," they replied. The old man sighed, looked around, made the sign of the cross over a church on a distant hill, laid down and died.

26. There would be no end to mistakes, if:
You acquire good books, but do not read them.
You read good books, but do not follow the advice they offer.
You follow the advice, but do it carelessly.
You meticulously follow the letter of the advice, but do not understand its essence.

27. It is enough to miss but a little and the needle does not get threaded.
It is enough to get lost in contemplation but a little and you miss your stop.
It is enough to be distracted but a little and bad thoughts make your head swim.
It is enough to move away from the Truth but a little and you will not find It any more.

28. To live a day in immortality and give your life for it,
would be worthy.
To breathe immortality for an hour and give your life for it,
would be worthy.
Even to inhale immortality for a second and give your life for it,
would be worthy.

Because if you taste immortality,
  you will never die.

29. When you encounter the long known,
  you are surprised by its novelty.
When you recognize the new in the long known,
  you are surprised by its depth.
When you discover the unperceived in what you have learned long ago,
  you are surprised by its infinity.
When you discover the imperceptibility of the infinite,
  you are surprised by how it cannot be expressed.

30. After putting on new clothes, one does not use the worn-out ones any more.
After building a new house, one does not live in the old one anymore.
When a new road is laid, the old one gets overgrown.
When the old heart dies, the new heart begins to live.

31. If you dig a pond, frogs will appear.
If you plant potatoes, weeds will grow too.
The more often you mow the grass, the thicker it grows.
The more you delve into this world, the more cares appear.

32. A woman and her little son once went to a toyshop. Near the shop, there was a bus stop and along the road there stood a concrete wall with a bright-colored mosaic that depicted dolphins playing in the waves. After a while, the woman wanted to buy a good holiday present for her son but she had forgotten where the toyshop that they had visited together was located. "My boy, do you remember the name of the bus stop by the toy shop?" she asked her son, just to be sure. "It is called "Dolphins," Mom!" the boy replied after some thinking. "Where do dolphins come from? There are no dolphins over there," the mother laughed. She looked into the directory and found the address of the toyshop. They came out of the bus at the familiar stop. "Look, Mom! The dolphins, I told you!" the boy pointed at the wall. "Here you go!" the mother smiled. "You were talking about this mosaic with dolphins?" "Mom, I don't know what it is called but I remembered the dolphins very well."

Mysterious Discourses

33. The husband came home from church. The wife asked him, "Was there anything interesting today?" "There was a very good sermon on how to be calm and solve all problems peacefully," the husband replied. "That sermon is just what you need!" the wife notes. "And, as usual, it is enough to say one word to you and you hear ten in return!" the husband says crossly. They stay silent for a moment, trying to think of some more caustic remarks and only then realize that someone kept ringing the doorbell. Guests come in. "It sounds like you were arguing. Why?" they ask the vexed couple. "Oh, it's nothing… We were just discussing today's sermon on calm and peacefulness you are supposed to use to approach all problems." "Judging by the noise, the more you talk about peace, the further away it goes from your house," the guests said.

34. If a mountain falls on you, it will not crush you,
    for you have already crushed yourself.
If the wind comes towards you, it will not bring you down,
    for you have already brought down yourself.
If fire burns you, it will not incinerate you,
    for you have already incinerated yourself.
If death looks for you, it will not find you,
    for you have already died and triumphed over it.

35. Trust in Him Who created trust.
Trust in Him Who has never erred.
He created trust precisely because He never errs.
He did not err in creating you, did He?

36. A married couple was returning to Moscow from Siberia by train. The journey took several days. Suddenly the husband fell ill on the way. He had a fever and became delirious. It appeared to the sick man that he was still in Siberia, in his native village. He could not understand why his bed kept shaking and why there was knocking outside. The wife tried to explain to him that he was in a train carriage but he did not hear her words. By morning, the man felt better. He calmed down and fell asleep. When he woke up, the train was at a station. His wife leaned over to him, "How are you feeling, dear?" she asked. "All right. I just cannot understand why my bed kept shaking and someone was knocking for so long outside the house." At that moment, the train started off and left the station. The recovering man looked through

the window in astonishment, "Where am I?" "My dear, you are on a train. You fell ill and had a fever. We are returning home from Siberia," the wife explained. "Now I get it," the husband sighed. "That's why I was so surprised. I just forgot that I had been on a train before I fell ill."

37. A man was spending the night in the forest. He had never heard an echo before. He lit a campfire, prepared something to eat and was getting ready to go to sleep but suddenly he heard the sound of stones falling in the nearby gorge. The man shouted towards the darkness, "Is anybody there?" "There, there, there…" he heard. "I wonder who it could possibly be," the man thought. "Are you near?" he asked out loud. "Near, near, near…" came the reply from the dark. "How on earth could someone be walking without light?" the man by the campfire thought, completely puzzled. "You have no light, do you?" he asked. "Do you, do you?.." sounded from the forest. "I need to help this poor fellow," the man thought, "And let him stay with me by the fire." So he replied aloud, "Come and rest here!" "Here, here, here…" the reply sounded. The man took a flashlight but, however hard he looked, there was nobody in the forest. "But there is no one!" the man exclaimed. "No one, no one…" the echo responded.

38. A man and his son cleared a plot of land surrounded by forest. They piled up the brush, made a brushwood fence, plowed up the soil and planted corn. When the corn began to ripen, they had to move to a thatched hut on the spot in order to guard the harvest from bears. The first night in the forest began. It was windy and cloudy. A bucket tinkled in the dark. "Dad, bears are here," the boy whispered. "No, son, that is the wind," the father assured him. In a while, strange shrieks sounded from the woods. "Dad, are those bears?" the boy asked. "No, son. That is an owl crying." "Dad, I keep thinking, how are we going to hear the bears? They walk very quietly." "Don't think too much, just listen carefully and that's it," the father said. Soon, the boy got tired of waiting for the bears' arrival and dozed off. But the father woke him up quietly, "Now listen carefully." They heard the crackle of the brushwood fence, then a rustle and then the sound of corn stalks being broken. "Now the real bears are here," the father replied and switched on his flashlight. A she-bear and two cubs ran out of the cornfield with great noise and escaped to the forest. "Let them run," the father smiled. "In a few days, we'll gather the harvest and leave them a little as a treat. Let them enjoy it."

Mysterious Discourses

39. An Artic explorer was asked to tell about the North Pole. He made himself comfortable in a chair and began, "Preparations are most important. It is important not to overlook anything, not to forget anything and to pack everything properly." "And the North Pole?" "Wait, we'll get to it. Then it is necessary to trace the correct route and to be able to identify your location." "This is clear. But could you please tell us about the Pole itself?" "Yes, yes. Just a moment. It must be said that blocks of ice moving are very dangerous, particularly in the night." "We have read about it in your books. Tell us about the Pole itself!" "Well, what could be said about it? The Pole looks the way it should look. That's it!"

40. Only children are able:
To forgive right away,
To live without money,
To have no desires,
To know nothing.

41. Bad thoughts cause bad desires.
Bad desires force one to commit bad deeds.
Tainted deeds spoil the mind.
A spoiled mind will never be able to conceive the Truth.

42. In olden times, in a town there lived an orphaned boy. His parents died when he was very little. The child was taken in by the neighbors. He lived with them and worked for them. One morning, loud drum beats and trumpets blaring sounded in the town. The boy ran towards the square and saw three heralds on splendid horses calling the people. One of them shouted, "Follow me and you will get rich!" "If you go with me," the second herald announced, "amazing adventures await you!" "Follow me," the third one exclaimed. "It is neither good nor bad where I shall lead you. But there, you will be like at your native home!" The confused people were running from one herald to another, not knowing which one to choose. The orphaned boy came close to the third herald and asked, "And what does it mean, 'like at home'?" And the herald leaned over to him from his saddle and whispered, "This means that they will love you there, little one." "Then I am with you!" the orphan said firmly.

43. A young man heard that it was necessary to be saved while you still live. He bought various books on salvation, read them and came to the conclusion that those

who gain salvation must be completely extraordinary people. That conclusion put him into dejection and confusion. "I am a long way from those people," he thought despondently. "But neither can I return to my old, entirely senseless life. So I shall go and ask experienced people for advice."

He came to hear different advice. Some were advising him to get married and not to preoccupy himself with difficult questions. Others were saying that in our times, one could no longer encounter people who gain salvation. Such people did exist, but it was long ago. Still others were teaching that it was necessary just to do good deeds and that was sufficient, while the issue of salvation was too lofty for comprehension. Thus, after asking various people for advice, the young man came to encounter a hermit living high up in the mountains. "Fear God, but also fear pride, if you truly want to be saved," the elder told him. "Cast away all your doubts and remember that the most ordinary man who had freed himself of all delusions and entirely turned to God, will be saved." "This means that even I can be saved?" rejoiced the young man. "Certainly! The Truth is open to all, but not all are open to the Truth. That is the key."

44. The older children tasted the jam that their mother had just made and they liked it a lot. Their little brother walked into the room, "May I also try the jam?" "Don't eat it, it is sour!" the older children joked. They ate some more of the sweet treat and ran outside. Mom looked into the room, "And why do not you taste the jam, my dear?" "Because it is sour!" the little boy replied tearfully. "It can't be true," Mom smiled. "Who told you that?" "The big brothers." "Oh, they were joking. Eat and don't doubt," the mother assured the boy. The older brothers ran inside again, "Why are you eating jam? It is sour!" they laughed. "No, it's sweet!" replied the boy. "Sweet? Where did you get that?" "Mom said so!" the boy replied with confidence.

45. There is nothing better than to choose the most unattractive apple of those offered.
There is nothing better than to prefer the last seat to all seats.
There is nothing better than to choose the worst conditions of life among all.
There is nothing better than to prefer humiliation to all honors.

46. When a bird tires in flight, it stops flapping its wings for a time.
When a skier tires of pushing off with his ski poles,

he gives himself a rest on the downward slope.
When a swimmer tires of swimming, he rests on the water.
When a man tires of his cares, he can rest only in prayer.

47. Just as you incessantly breathe,
Just as your heart incessantly beats,
Just as your blood incessantly flows in your veins,
So you must incessantly strive for the Truth, as long as you live.

48. A man was sitting on a bench in his garden reading a book. A beautiful bird came flying by and sat on a branch. The man started to admire it. Another bird, equally beautiful also flew near. A third bird, exactly like the first two arrived and sat on the branch next to them. The man was looking at them in rapture. But then a whole flock of those birds that were circling nearby noticed the three birds on the tree, flew up to them and began to take seats on the branches with much noise and brawl. The man frowned, sighed, closed the book and went into the house.

49. If you look for yourself on a map, you will never find it.
If you ask your acquaintances to show which one of them is you,
    they will make fun of you.
If you try to open your house with keys to another, you will never succeed.
If in your sleep you wait to be awoken by the people you are dreaming about,
    you will never awake in time.

50. This world lives in such a way that:
If you should wish to pick a blade of grass, you may cut your hand.
If you should wish to walk off the path, you may hurt your foot and stumble.
If you should wish to look up, you may lose your way.
If you should wish to look back, you may lose what you have gained.

51. He who looks into the sky sees the clouds fly by.
He who looks into the sea sees the ships sail.
He who looks into the distance sees the snow-covered summits.
He who is able not to look anywhere will see himself.

52. A grown-up grandson came to his native village to see his grandparents. He had not seen them for many years and had not written to them. He remembered them somehow and pitied them, so he went to see how they were doing. He approached the house and noticed that the yard was overgrown with weeds, the shutters were nailed closed and on the door there was a lock. He walked around and looked inside through the cracked shutters. Of course, no one was inside. A neighbor saw him and asked, "Are you not the grandson of the old folks?" "I am." "Don't look for them, they are no more. They passed away two years ago. As for the keys, I have them, so you can go into the house and see what it's like." The grandson took the keys, threw open the shutters and went inside. The house was empty. Only the photographs remained hanging. Grandpa and Grandma still looked alive in them. The grandson sat down on a stool and thought, "What do I really keep looking for? I'll stay here." The neighbor knocked at the door, came in and asked, "Well, have you made up your mind?" "I've made up my mind to stay." "That's good. The main thing is to be a man." "That's right. A man is exactly what I want to become," said the grandson.

53. A man heard that there was Truth in the world; so, he went looking for it. Once, he sees Lie walking towards him. "Where are you heading?" Lie asks. "I am searching for Truth." "Very well," Lie says. "I would also like to see Truth at least once, as I have never met it. Let's go together." They came to a city and asked, "Is Truth here?" "It was here, but it left. Where it went, we do not know." The man and Lie went further. They came to another city and asked again, "Was Truth here?" "Yes, it was," they replied to them. "It is still walking somewhere near. And who is that with you?" "This is Lie," the man responded. "But who on earth can find Truth together with Lie?" the people ask, puzzled. "You have to chase away Lie first." "You must be right," says the man. So he chased Lie away, looked, and saw Truth itself walking towards him already. "Hello, good man," it said. What a wonder!

54. If you meet your mother after a long separation, you will not leave her, will you?
If you see your father whom you parted with in your youth,
  you will not abandon him, will you?
If your son returns to you after a quarrel, you will not turn away from him, will you?
If after a long quest the heart encounters the Truth,
  it will not be able to live on without It, will it?

Mysterious Discourses

55. When they praise you, you are pleased,
    and when they curse you, you are hurt, but is there Truth in it?
When they give you presents, you are pleased,
    and when they take them away, you are hurt, but is there Truth in it?

56. Where is the joyful boy you were in your childhood?
Where is the enthusiastic youngster you were in your youth?
Where is the man unsatisfied with life you were in your maturity?
Where is the silent old man you were in your old age?

57. The larger the leak in a boat is, the harder it is to sail.
The stronger the heart is attached to pleasures,
    the less it understands the meaning of life.

58. The further you go, the more you get lost.
The more you ask, the less you learn.
The more you search, the more you get muddled.
The sooner you return, the more you find.

59. A man bought a plot of land but it turned out that the land was bad. He sold it and bought another one but it turned out that there was no water on it. He sold that plot too and bought a new one. The land was so-so but the water was bad. The man got sad and neglected the land. Another man bought a rocky plot with a little water that no one wanted to buy. He began to throw out the stones, day by day, until he threw them all out. He cleared the spring and had water enough and to spare. He planted vines and now he is eating grapes and offering them to others.

60. You look from afar, It appears more or less clear.
You come closer, and It is hardly clear.
You stand near, nothing is at all clear.
You come inside, there is even nothing to say...
And It is what It is.

61. It is good to find your own house in this world.
It is good to find your own room in that house.

SILENCE OF THE HEART

It is good to find yourself in that room.
It is good to find in yourself the One who created all that.

62. To live with bad thoughts in the heart is like walking a scorching road on a sultry day, dying of thirst.
To chase bad thoughts from the heart with prayer is like finding refuge in the shade of a tree after walking in the heat and discovering a spring with clear fresh water.

63. Even a cat when it is hunting for a mouse can teach vigilance to a man who is striving to clear his heart.
Even a child when he is learning to walk can teach patience to a man who is striving to master prayer.

64. Don't bring back into your house the rubbish you have already thrown out.
Don't seek a meeting with a person who has caused you much harm.
Don't incur big debts again if you have already repaid them.
Don't return to the evil you have already freed your heart from.

65. You work from dawn to dusk, breaking your back, return to a rented room, fall down on the bed. You have no strength left to raise your head, let alone to cook dinner. You sigh with a moan: no family, no home. What is all this fuss for? Where will you find rest?

Money keeps flowing in, you are promoted again and again and you actually don't work too hard. Business seems to run itself. But your wife looks unhappy, your children shun you like wolf cubs, you have no more close friends and ahead there is emptiness. You cannot fall asleep till morning. What is all this fuss for? Where will you find rest?

66. The body light like air,
The blue sky like the eyes of a child,
The meadows like green fluff,
The flowers like a splendid carpet,
The rainbow afar like the smile of the earth,

Mysterious Discourses

Can all that be possible?
Yes, if you yourself become available for such a world.

67. Calm the sea and you will sail peacefully.
Tame the thunderstorm and you will walk without fear.
Stop the lightning and you will not be afraid to look into the sky.
Calm the heart and all worries will be left behind.

68. A farmer decided to find water on his plot of land. He noted where the grass was most lush, took a spade and started digging a ditch, hoping to run into water in such a way. He dug a long ditch. The soil was moist indeed but there was no water in sight. Then he saw an old man walking by shaking his head. "Grandpa, am I doing something wrong?" the farmer asked. "You are, son. You should have asked how to find water before you started digging." "Help me, Grandpa," the man asked. "Son, you should fill up your ditch first. Then start digging into the ground there, where you started. This way you'll find what you are looking for." The farmer thanked the old man, filled the ditch back in with soil and began to dig where he had started. He did not dig for long before he found water. He was very glad.

69. A rumor circulated that somewhere in a long-abandoned house a treasure was hidden. A lot of people went there, broke the stove, tapped the walls through and through and rummaged in the basement but found nothing. Then they dug up the garden, nothing. So they quit trying. Once, a traveler stopped for the night in the abandoned house. Everywhere there was rubbish, dust and pieces of bricks. So he cleared a corner where he could lie down and decided to hang his bag on the wall, out of the reach of mice. He picked up a rusty nail, set it against the wall, hit it and saw the nail go into the wall completely. He tapped around and felt that there was a hollow in the wall. He knocked off the plaster, took out a brick and realized it was a cache. He put his hand inside and took out an iron box. Inside of it were gold coins. The man shook his head in surprise. He waited for morning and brought the gold to the authorities. They were astonished. So many had searched for that treasure and could not find it and that man had found it without searching! And they were even more amazed that he had brought the treasure to them instead of taking it himself. "What reward do you want for this treasure?" they asked the traveler. "I don't want anything. This stuff is not mine. I just want permission to build a church

with my own hands at a place that I choose. This is the reward I want." "And that's it? Build!" they told him. "What an odd man you are!"

70. A boy ran up to his grandfather who was sitting in an armchair, "Granddad, what is patience?" "Patience is when all your teeth fall out." "I see." "This is when your eyesight gets poor." "That's clear too." "Patience is when you no longer hear well." "And what else?" "Patience is also when you can hardly walk and are ill all the time." "Then patience is you, Granddad! And I am still little, I am far from it." "No, dear grandson. If you don't have patience in your youth, you may not reach even my age."

71. The grandfather liked to stay alone for long periods of time. He would spend entire days in his armchair. And even when darkness fell, he remained there frequently forgetting to turn off the light. His son would come into the room, the daughter-in-law would glance inside and his grandchildren would run in. He said nothing and only smiled at them. "Dad, maybe you would like to read something? Here are some books, newspapers and magazines. Are you not bored alone?" the son asked him. "No, my dear," the father replied. "It's already hard for me to read and I am not at all bored staying alone." "Why, Dad?" "Old age is an amazing and beautiful time. Only in his old age does man begin to understand something about life and then it is time to die. So, as soon as you understand life, there is nothing left for you to do on earth." "But we wouldn't want you to leave us," the son said sadly. "And I wouldn't want you to keep me in this life," his father said with a calm and gentle smile.

72. At night, when we take a lamp and shine it into the distance,
   we shall see all that surrounds us.
And if we shine that lamp into our faces,
   we shall see only the light and shall be unable to discern anything around.

73. When the play is over, the curtain is dropped.
When the reading is finished, the book is closed.
When man dies, he is buried.
When the Truth is realized, all sorrows end.

74. There is no wind and not a single leaf moves on a tree.
There are no people and not a single sound is heard in the house.

Mysterious Discourses

There are no cares and the world becomes beautiful.
There is no memory of the world and the heart becomes akin to the sky.

75. A young man with a broken leg was brought to the hospital in an ambulance. When he was carried on a stretcher, the nurse told him, "Don't be upset, you will recover your leg quickly." "To the contrary, I am glad that they brought me to a hospital. What would I do at home alone with a broken leg?" The nurse only shrugged her shoulders. They fixed the man's leg and put it in plaster. A few days later, the nurse told the young man, "Good news for you. We are discharging you from the hospital. Now you will continue the treatment at your place." And he replied, "Not good news for me. I live alone. The elevator does not work. So I have nothing to be happy about." The nurse just shrugged her shoulders. Then she thought a little and said, "You are hard to please. When they bring you in, you are glad and when they discharge you, you are upset." "No, it is you who are hard to please," the patient replied. "When I am glad, you are upset and when I am upset, you are glad. Actually...what is your name?" The nurse blushed and said, "No, now I am not glad...or, rather, not upset." What happened next – we don't know.

76. It happens that a heavy storm roots out colossal trees.
It happens that a ravine in the mountains turns a rapid river into a big quiet lake.

77. Don't keep at home a dog that bites everyone.
Don't keep in the heart thoughts that judge everyone.

78. A family living in Tashkent, capital of Uzbekistan, came to see their elderly relatives in a distant Siberian village. They brought big Central Asian grapes as a present. "What is this?" said the old folks, surprised. "This? Ordinary grapes," the guests said. The old folks carefully took a grape each and tried to peel it. "You shouldn't do that," the visitors smiled. "Grapes are not peeled, you eat them just like that." The old folks distrustfully ate a grape each and exclaimed, "This is a wonder!" "No wonder. Just simple grapes," the guests laughed. "Simple for you but for us, it is a real wonder," the old folks said.

79. In the old days, it happened that a heated stove in a village house was closed too early. Gradually, charcoal fumes began to fill the room undetected. Sometimes, entire families got poisoned that way.

SILENCE OF THE HEART

Just so, if the heart, unaware, accumulates cunning, bad thoughts and does not confess them, it dies spiritually and it is very difficult then to help the man.

80. A peasant bought a young, ill-trained horse. He tied it to a peg and left it to graze in a meadow. He came back in the evening and saw that the horse had untied itself. The master ran after the horse and the horse ran away from the master, through brush and across ravines. The peasant ran and ran after it and got terribly tired. Then he thought, "Why am I running after it at all? Let it run after me." He went into the house, took a piece of bread with salt, sat down in the meadow and started to eat slowly. Soon, he heard the brush crackle. The horse was edging through the thicket. Finally, it came out of the brush, stirring its ears and wagging its nostrils. The bread was near! At last, it came up to the man, stretched its muzzle towards the bread and started neighing faintly. The master could not help laughing. "You little fool," he said. "All right, eat the bread." He threw the halter on the horse and led it home and so they became friends.

81. If your clothes get drenched,
   don't lament over the rain, take an umbrella.
If your hands are cold,
   don't blame the frost, put on gloves.
If it hurts you to hear bad things about yourself,
   don't complain about people, try to become better.
If it seems to you that everything around is bad,
   blame yourself for having little patience.

82. Lie deviates and Truth acts straightforwardly.
Lie takes cover and Truth does not hide.
Lie wants to resemble Truth and Truth is always the way it is.
Lie cannot live without Truth and Truth lives not having need of anything.

83. To change your life and get rid of bad habits is okay.
To stop doing bad deeds is good.
To reject bad desires is even better.
To forswear bad thoughts is the best.

84. A step back towards your own self,
   is better than a thousand steps forward leading to nothing.
To look inside yourself a single time,
   is better than to travel the whole world and understand nothing.

85. You strained your foot. It may heal.
You fell down the stairs and were hurt. You may get cured.
You got hit by a car. You may survive.
But if passions have taken possession of you,
   it is much worse than to strain your foot, fall downstairs and get hit by a car.

86. A young man tried many professions without success while his father had worked his entire life as a simple gardener. Disappointed because of his failures, the young man had no idea what else he could try doing and was restless. When he was sitting at home in sadness, his mother came up to him and said with sympathy, "Misfortune again, son?" "Yes, Mom. I guess I just don't have any talents. That's why I don't know what I should do." "Do you want me to give you some advice?" the mother asked. "Yes, Mom." "It is very simple," she said. "Work in the garden like your father and listen to what he tells you. Believe me, this is quite enough to be happy." "Mom, it seems to me it is too simple," the young man objected. "Happiness is always simple, son," the mother said with a smile.

87. Know that you lost if:
You replied to a reproach with but a single word,
You said but a single word to justify yourself,
You pronounced but a single word of reproof.
You let in but a single bad thought.

88. The country to which you must sail is across the sea.
The city to which you must go is across the river.
The house that you must reach is across the street.
The room that you must enter is in front of you.

89. An entrepreneur very much liked quiet. For the sake of it, he sold his small noisy factory, settled in the countryside and bought a farm. But on the farm, there were many noise-producing machines: tractors, generators and compressors. The man

kept looking for quiet in the most distant rooms of his house but could find it nowhere. In the end, he bought special noise-blocking headphones but even they did not help much. Once, a friend from the city came to see him. Right off the bat, the host began to complain, trying to speak above the sound of the lawnmower, "See, I came here for the quiet and it is nowhere to be found! I am wearing headphones but they do not help much!" "Have all the work on the farm done strictly on a schedule," the guest advised. "Then the quiet will appear by itself and you will not have to look for it." Half a year passed and a letter came from the farmer. "Thank you very much, my friend!" he wrote. "Now I hear the birds sing. I no longer wear the headphones. When it gets quiet, the quiet comes by itself."

90. Do not imitate the young, if you are not young,
the strong, if you are not strong,
the clever, if you are not clever,
and the rich, if you are not rich.

Be yourself, and that is sufficient to be,
Young, if you are not young,
Strong, if you are not strong,
Clever, if you are not clever,
and rich, if you are not rich.

91. An old fisherman was walking along the bank of a river. He had a bucket full of fish he had just caught. Suddenly, the fisherman saw a fishing rod stuck in the ground and a man in the water by the float. "What happened, did your hook snag on something?" the fisherman asked him. "No," he replied. "I am driving the fish to the bait." The old man just shook his head, "What an odd fellow! Doing this, you will only scare them away. The fish will see the bait itself." "And what should I do then?" the beginner fisherman asked. "You must observe the float from the bank. The less noise you make the better. This is my advice to you."

92. If a beautiful tree with marvelous fruit curing every illness were to grow in an arid desert, it would not be as astonishing as what a man can gain in himself.
If an amazingly beautiful and bright child were to be born to an elderly childless couple, it would not be as joyous as the joy of what can be born in a man's heart.

93. A man came to see his friend who was ill. He greeted the friend and asked how he was feeling. "What? What?" the sick friend replied. "How are you feeling?" the visitor said louder. "I am ill and I don't know what's wrong with me. It seems that it is something terrible because I don't want to see or hear anything," the friend responded. But the guest noticed that his friend looked well and did not give the impression of being terribly sick. "Maybe it's just your impression? Possibly, you are just in a bad mood and that's all," he said. "No, no! It's some serious illness. We want to send for an experienced practitioner." "I see," the guest said pensively. He decided to test how serious his friend's illness was. "Listen," he whispered to his hearing-impaired friend. "Why is all that money lying in the corner there?" "Where, where? Show me!" the sick friend responded with vigor, jumping up from the bed. "Sorry, it's a mistake," the guest laughed. "But as far as you being completely healthy, I already don't doubt it at all!"

94. If they give you dirt, you will not take it, will you?
If they tell you foul words, you will not listen to them, will you?
If they offer you a false teaching, you will not accept it, will you?
If disgusting thoughts seduce you, you will not follow them, will you?

95. Two acquaintances met in a park. Each of them had a dog on a leash. The owner of the first dog began to praise its merits, "When I go shopping," he said, "It carries my wallet in its teeth and no one dares to take it away." "That's good," the owner of the second dog said. "And my dog buys its feed itself and no one dares not give it the change." "Why?" "Because I am standing alongside."

96. Bees do not know scientific data on honey,
  but they know how to make it.
Martins do not know aerodynamics,
  but they know how to fly.
A child does not know the meaning of life,
  but he can live wiser than adults.

97. Members of a naturalist society were preparing for a mountain hike in the Caucasus. One of them bought a book on the rare species of that area. They were leafing through it, exchanging remarks. "Well, some data are just frightening," one of the tourists noted. "It says here that one may encounter rabid foxes in the forest." "Oh,

this is nothing compared with what is to come," replied another naturalist. "Here it says that wolves, too, may be rabid!" The members of the society exchanged glances and began to think. "And here is the most shocking!" yet another naturalist said, pointing at a page. "Deer can also develop rabies! Truly, an encounter with such a deer on a path is not for those with weak nerves!" The naturalists unilaterally resolved to burn the ominous book. The mountain hike did not take place.

98. It is hard to describe:
The amazement of a son, who had long been keeping on a shelf a stone left by his
    father, when it became known that it was a gold nugget.
The emotion of an art collector, who had long been keeping at home a plain painting,
    that unexpectedly turned out to be the work of a great artist.
The feeling of a man, who had spent his entire life looking for the Truth,
    that in the end opened up in his heart by itself.

99. A hidden video surveillance system was installed in a factory. Its control panel was located in a small room by the entrance. The operator could see and hear everyone who was passing through the entrance but he himself remained invisible behind a two-way mirror. The curious employees gazed at the glass and everyone was voicing their remarks. "It's obvious there's no one there," some said. "If there was a man in the room, we would be able to see him. Isn't that right?" "Actually, there is not even a room there," others stated. "They just glazed a part of the entrance with plate glass. That's it." And still others were confident that the false rumors about the new surveillance system and the operator were being spread on purpose to scare the employees. The operator himself, listening to all this talk and seeing the futile attempts of the curious to find out the Truth, only smiled.

100. If you could not rein yourself in when you were young,
    when would you take the right way?
If you could not master your maturity,
    when would you have time to make the right choice?
If you are unable to hold onto your old age,
    when will you ever do it?

Chapter Seven
One with God

Cares tie the hands.
Anxiety ties the mind.
Worries tie the heart.
Only the Truth unties all knots.

1. In order to solve the question of life and death, you need:
To make an effort like a man struggling underwater, short of air and trying to surface.
To value time like a man who has learned that he is fatally ill and still has so much to complete.
To try to get rid of ignorance like a man who is seeing a horrible nightmare and trying his very best to wake up.

2. A little fish is asking its Mom, "How can I save myself from the fishermen's nets? Must I dive deeper?" "You will not have enough time," Mom replied. "The net is lowered too quickly." "Maybe I can come to the surface and jump over the net?" the young fish asked, not losing hope. "Then you will be caught by seagulls." "How can I be saved then?" "The best is to try to avoid the places where the fishermen cast their nets," said the Mom with a sigh.

3. It is sad when we hold onto our parents and they leave us.
It is sad when we hold onto passions and they kill us.
It is sad when we hold onto life and it deserts us.

4. Leave understanding to others and you will understand everything yourself.
Leave knowledge to others and you will know everything yourself.
Leave happiness to others and happiness will find you itself.
Leave wisdom to others and the Truth will never part from you.

Mysterious Discourses

5. He who set out on the journey and came back right away will know both the hardships of the road and the disappointment of not having attained his goal.
He who stopped half way is better than the one who never departed at all.
He who stopped a little short of the goal is better than the one who stopped half way.
He who walked all the way to the end may return to share the hardships of the road with those who have no strength left to walk on.

6. You don't find the first ray of the rising sun,
it reaches you itself when you stay awake.
You don't find the Truth,
It reaches you Itself when you are trying to find It.

7. If you have found a purse with money,
it is better to find the one who has lost it.
If you have taken another man's treasure,
it will surely leave you.
Your treasure, if you find it,
will have no other owner but you.

8. To know how to acquire, you must learn to sacrifice.
To know what love is, one must also learn what hate is.
To know how to live, you must learn to die.

9. A large group of people in dark spectacles entered an art gallery. All of them were staying together, not moving away from each other a single step. The guide approached them and began to speak about the painting in front of which they had stopped, "This work of the great master..." But the people in spectacles were not looking at the painting that she was telling them about. "Please don't get distracted," the guide asked. "And listen with attention. Now I shall tell you about the life of the great artist who created this immortal work..." Gradually she began to notice that at least one man, whom in fact, the entire group was following, was listening to her carefully and studying all the paintings. The guide came up to the man and said, "Your group is really strange. Except for you, no one is interested in what I am saying." "Oh, sorry, I should have warned you in advance," the man said, embarrassed. "I am accompanying a group of people with heavily impaired vision and hearing. They just want to be in an art gallery to feel what it is like."

10. Once a poor man had an amazing dream. He dreamed that his right hand was endowed with a miraculous quality. Everything he pointed at with his right hand would vanish. An unfamiliar voice in his dream said that he would be able to use the magic only three times. After waking up, the poor man decided to test if his dream would come true. He walked the streets of the city for a long time, not knowing at what to point until he saw a shackled prisoner being led for execution by armed guards. The emaciated prisoner raised his arms towards the sky and moaned, "Will anyone in this world pity me, the unfortunate one? I am innocent and they are leading me to the scaffold." The poor man believed the sincere words of the prisoner and, engulfed by pity for him, pointed at his shackles with his right hand. To his astonishment, the shackles vanished and the prisoner broke away and escaped. The guards seized the poor man and, threatening him with their swords, began to accuse him of breaking the law. The poor man, frightened, pointed with his right hand at the swords and they vanished too. The guards became infuriated and dragged the unfortunate poor man to the High Sheriff. "This is the one who is the rabble-rouser!" they shouted. "You shall be executed in the place of the prisoner who escaped!" "Me?" the poor man, amazed, poked into his chest with his right hand…and vanished before everybody's eyes.

11. A ski jump competition was taking place. A reporter from a leading newspaper was interviewing one of the winners, "Sir, in this manly and dangerous sport, the main thing must be to bring yourself to jump?" "No," the athlete replied. "The main thing is to land."

12. A mother asked her son to go and buy some milk. The boy grabbed the milk can and, without even looking inside, ran to the shop. The milkman opened the can and shook his head, "Son, there is some old milk left at the bottom." "I am sorry. I did not notice," the boy blushed. "It's all right, just be more attentive next time," the milkman said to the boy. "Now wash the milk can well and I shall pour some fresh milk for you." "And why must I wash it? There will be milk in the can anyway, right? Maybe I should just pour out the old milk and that's it?" "No. If you mix the fresh milk with the old, it will turn sour quickly. This way, you'll never bring fresh milk home."

13. Everything that your eyes see will disappear some time.
But what they do not see will never disappear.

Mysterious Discourses

Everything that you hold will slip from your hands some time.
But the hands that you know not, meet you at birth and take you home at death.

14. A grandmother with her two grandsons went to take a walk in the city park. The younger grandson hid behind the monument for Pushkin, a well-known, deceased Russian poet. "And where might the grandson be?" the grandmother asked, losing sight of the boy. At that instant the boy looked out from behind the monument. "Over there, Grandma," the older grandson said, pointing at him. But the little boy hid behind the statue again. "No, I don't see anyone," the old woman said. "How can you see him, if he hid behind Pushkin?" "What do you mean 'behind Pushkin?'" the grandmother said, amazed. "Behind the Pushkin monument, Grandma," the grandson laughed.

15. The warehouse of a store selling weed and pest killer was located across from a residential building. When a truck was being loaded, a sack with sulfur broke and yellow powder scattered on the ground. Children ran up. "What a pretty kind of sand!" they rejoiced. But at that moment the yard-keeper appeared and began sweeping the sulfur up with a broom, looking cross. "No, no. Don't do that!" the children shouted. "We are going to play here!" "No, children!" the yard-keeper replied sternly. "Poison is not a toy for you. It is better not to touch it at all and to take it away from our yard the faster the better. And now get yourselves home to wash your hands, quickly!"

16. A hare ran into the forest in wintertime to eat some bark from the young trees. The wolf noticed the hare and chased it. The hare ran and ran and escaped into the fields. The wolf reached the edge of the forest and was afraid to run further. "No," it thought, "I'll not run across the fields. There is nothing there, nowhere to hide." So, the wolf went back into the forest. And the hare kept running at full speed rejoicing. "All the same, to live in the forest is not for me. The fields are much better: freedom, open space, no trees, no bushes, no anything. Here it's easy to run away from the wolf."

17. A politician was on trial. They asked him, "Why did you not allow people to leave the country?" "So that they would not get spoiled," he replied. "And why did you eliminate so many people?" "For the sake of order," he said. "And why did you start the war?" "So that there would be peace." "But what need did you have of other

countries?" "I wanted to help." "Indeed?" the judges said. "This is absolute Truth!" the politician insisted. "Not a single word of this man is to be believed," the judges concluded and passed a sentence according to his deeds.

18. A young entomologist once read about an extraordinarily rare and beautiful butterfly with a splendid pattern on its wings. He decided to find it at any cost. But, whomever he asked, no one knew exactly where the butterfly could be found. At last, the young man met an old colleague who had been fortunate enough to see the beautiful creature. He gave the young man some advice, "In order to find this rare butterfly, you must go to a small distant country and search for an equally rare tropical plant. The butterfly prefers the flowers of that plant to all others. When you find it, you must wait for the blossoming time, hide nearby and keep your eyes on the flower. When the butterfly comes and descends upon the flower, be extremely cautious. Don't scare it away. The main thing is not to miss the moment when it spreads its marvelous wings, the beauty of which few people have seen. To find the flower is within your power. But to see the butterfly come, the following year, ten years later or at the end of your life, that depends only on your faith and determination."

19. No one likes spoiled fruit.
No one likes disorder in his house.
No one likes dirt on his clothes.
Why would you keep thought garbage in your heart?

20. A young man heard of a mysterious magic grass that can resurrect the dead. He came to an elder living in seclusion in the woods who knew where to look for the grass. The elder listened to the young man and said, "Yes, I know where that grass grows but it is guarded by three evil giants. The first of them is as tall as a high tree and very nimble. The second is as big as a mountain but clumsy. The third giant's head reaches the clouds but he is the slowest of all. Know that they are your murderers. You must fight with them and triumph over them. Otherwise they will kill you, just as they killed a multitude of daring men who have challenged them in the past. If you first destroy the swiftest and the nimblest one, it will be easier to overcome the others." "How can I possibly triumph over them?" the young man asked. "Only through contempt for death," the elder responded firmly. "I do not fear death," the brave young man replied. "Then listen to me carefully," the elder said, looking him right in the eyes. "There is only one way to destroy the terrible giants

Mysterious Discourses

but it is open only to a brave heart. So remember, you can kill the first giant by contempt for his concepts, the second by contempt for his intentions and the third by contempt for his false frightening mirages." "I understand the sense of your counsel and thank you!" the young man exclaimed. Full of courage, he went to take possession of the magic grass. His venture met with success and he brought life back to all the people killed by the three evil giants.

21. If you know the magician's secrets,
    his tricks will not deceive you.
If you know how to safeguard your heart,
    thoughts will not delude you.

22. Cares tie the hands.
Anxiety ties the mind.
Worries tie the heart.
Only the Truth unties all knots.

23. When there is no fuss inside, there is attention.
If attention is not distracted, it is becoming like crystal, pure and complete.
Crystal clear attention is not split, it is like solid rock.

24. He who makes the first step and does not get frightened:
Will cross the stormy sea,
Will not be harmed, having fallen into the executioners' hands,
Will come out of any prison and regain freedom,
Will fearlessly pass through the gates of death.
He will learn on his own how it happens.

25. Stop dreaming and all your dreams will come true.
Stop desiring and all your desires will be fulfilled.
Stop being stingy and you will be rich.
Stop being envious and you will always rejoice.

26. In your youth, all roads appear short,
    in old age, they appear long.

In your youth, life appears endless,
   in old age, it is akin to an instant.

27. The further you go out of the thicket, the easier it becomes to walk.
The lower you descend from the mountains, the more even the road gets.
The more you free yourself of vain thoughts, the clearer the goal of life becomes.
The more the heart is purified, the more the Truth reveals itself.

28. You pursue Life, and It retreats.
You go away from Life, and It follows you.
You stop, and It appears near.
You patiently wait, not losing hope, and that Life becomes yours.

29. If you walk all the earth,
   you will still never come to yourself.
If you acquire all knowledge and study all science,
   you will still never comprehend yourself.
But if you are able to leave all,
   then you will begin to understand that which is in you.

30. The children woke up early in the morning. There was silence in the house. A ray of sun, having penetrated through the loosely shut curtains in the nursery, formed a freakish drawing of a wolf with its ears stirring and teeth bared upon a wall. "A wolf has come up to our house," the children whispered. "It is probably looking in the window and this is its shadow." "Grandma once said that the wolf would not eat those who put their heads under the blankets," one of the children remembered. All of the children covered themselves with their blankets right away and none of them dared to get up. Steps sounded, then the door opened and their mother came into the room. "And why are you still in bed, little sleepyheads?" she asked merrily. "Mom, a wolf is outside the window!" the children answered together. The mother drew the curtains apart. Sunlight was flowing into the room through the foliage of the big maple tree. "Look out the window. Your fears are just imaginary. There is no wolf by the house. A ray of sun comes through the leaves and draws on the wall a shadow that looks like a wolf." The children rushed towards the window, "Yes, Mom! There is no wolf, but on the wall it looks real!" "This wolf will not eat anyone, my dears," the mother said with a smile.

Mysterious Discourses

31. A newborn infant is not able to tell anything about his mother to other infants. A sleeping man is not able to tell anyone about his dream until he wakes up. A diver underwater is not able to tell anything about what he sees to other divers.

32. Wherever you look, there is quiet, boundless sea. It is close to dead calm. The sky is cloudless. The sun rises slowly on the horizon. A coffin is floating on the sea, tossing slightly. Two shipwreck survivors in the water are struggling for their lives. There is nothing to cling to and they are already terribly fatigued. They notice the coffin and do not know what to do. It is scary to cling to it but they do not want to drown. Finally, they make an effort and reach the coffin. "You are not shocked by what we are clinging to?" one of the men asks. "No," the other one replies. "I am more shocked by what might be inside."

33. Three digits met: the Ten, the Hundred and the Thousand and began to talk. "They say that if you foreswear what you have, you will receive more," the Ten shared the news. "Not bad," replied the Hundred. "But let someone show an example." "True. Of anyone, I have something to leave for my children," agreed the Thousand. "Although I worked hard to earn my zero," the Ten said. "Let me be the first." So the Ten threw away the zero and became One. "So how are you feeling now?" the digits asked. "Wonderful. Complete freedom." Having heard that answer, the Hundred also cast away the zeros and became One. The two Ones embraced. "Let us see what the fat boy is going to do." The Thousand turned and twisted but what was there to do? To be alone is still worse. So the Thousand braced up and cast away the zeros. "It is really much easier to live without zeros," the Thousand rejoiced. "That's the point," the three Ones said to each other. "It turns out that without the zeros we are all One… It seems funny knowing how we boasted of our zeros to one another. Only now, after we relinquished them, we finally realize that zero is nothing."

34. Three travelers were riding in a car on a highway. "A city!" one of them exclaimed with surprise and pointed into the distance. "And it looks medieval somehow!" "There can be no city here," replied his friend, who was at the wheel. "I know this area well." "And there were no road signs of any kind," said the third traveler, puzzled. The travelers decided to get closer to the old city and turned onto a side road. The farther they went on it, the more they were bewildered. A real medieval city and in their time was looming up in front of them. Suddenly, they came to a

barrier. A most ordinary watchman was sitting in a most ordinary booth. "This is simply amazing!" the travelers kept exclaiming. "Where on earth did all these ancient buildings come from?" "There is nothing amazing here," the watchman grumbled, coming out of the booth. "They are going to make a movie here, that's why they fashioned all these props."

35. The white lily. If it is revealed to you what it signifies, that will be beautiful. He who understands this will also understand all the rest.

36. Where is that man who is able to stop?
Where is that man who can turn back?
Where is that man who can start anew?

All doors are open to him on this way, if only he appears! But he does not stop, does not turn back and stubbornly continues to commit the same mistakes. He opens other doors and goes away in a different direction from whence there is no return.

37. If you live in some country, leave it.
If you live in some city, go away from it.
If you live in some house, abandon it.

If you think that you understood this advice,
    think again and find that only place where you must live.

38. From afar, it looks like an impregnable fortress.
Should you come closer, it is like a safe refuge.
If you stand near, you will see nothing external.
And if you come inside, you will find nothing internal.

And still...it is not what people call "Life" and not what people call "Death."

39. Purer than the highest summits,
Purer than the purest lakes,
Purer than the purest skies,
The purity of the human heart, in its depths, is deeper than all depths.

Mysterious Discourses

40. Hide it more securely, that is precisely where they will look.
Go further away, that is precisely where they will come.

Offer your help to all, and you will only hinder everyone.
Start to care for all, and people will begin to flee from you.

41. He who deals with aromas is always fragrant.
He who abides in the Truth always manifests it.

42. Residents of one country from time immemorial revered venomous snakes. Those people found baby snakes, brought them to their homes, fed them and took care of them until they turned into big snakes whose bite was deadly. At some point, the snakes attacked their keepers, bit them and they died in terrible agony. Nevertheless, all the people thought that everything was the way it should be, what else?

Once, a traveler came to the land of the snake venerators. He knew nothing of the strange local customs. He asked the people, "Why do you revere the snakes that kill you?" "Because they are our best friends. We always carry them upon ourselves and warm them with our body heat." "But they destroy you!" exclaimed the stranger, amazed by the locals' strange attachment. "But we have become accustomed to them and cannot live without them." "It's clear to me," the traveler said with sadness. "Neither can you live without them, nor can you live long with them."

43. A traveler met a man on a forest path. He noticed on the man's chest a big swollen leech and hurried to caution the unfortunate man. "Hey, friend! You should take this leech off your chest right away, otherwise it will suck all your blood out!" "This is not a leech. This is my blood brother," came the strange reply. "He is always with me. Wherever I go, he goes too. And I have no one closer than him. He is dearer to my heart than my father and mother." The traveler sighed and said, "That depends. Blood brother to some, blood enemy to others."

44. Pity your neighbor, don't slander him,
   and you will be yourself.
Do not give in to lust, be chaste,
   and you will be yourself.
Do not consent to bad thoughts, clear your heart from them,

and you will be yourself.
Do not despair, safeguard the peace of your soul,
and you will be yourself.

45. They invited a repairman to a bakery because a bread-making machine had broken down. The vexed baker began to explain to the repairman, "This unit stopped obeying me. Now, one part of it is operating, now another, now all of them start working and all in the wrong mode." The repairman examined the machine and said, "We are going to switch off one part of the unit after another. Then we shall adjust all the parts and connect them in the right order. I am sure that the unit is going to work fine after that!" Together with the baker, they fixed the machine and it began making good bread. Wiping his hands with a towel, the repairman told the baker, "The trick is to connect everything correctly and in the right sequence." "And to bake good bread is an even greater trick!" the baker added.

46. When all bad thoughts are expelled from the heart,
stillness falls upon it.
When you take upon your shoulders the burden of the suffering of all people,
you will see the Divine Countenance in your heart.

47. A man and his son read a book on hypnosis and decided to conduct an experiment. The father said to the boy, "Son, you must mentally picture one of our family members and command them to come here." "Okay, Dad," the son said. A prolonged silence followed. "Whom are you trying to summon?" the father whispered. The boy replied, also in a whisper. "I keep repeating to myself, 'Dad, appear! Dad, appear!'" "But how can I appear if I am already here?" the father asked. "Great!" the son exclaimed. "This means our experiment succeeded!"

48. When the husband found out that his wife was to give birth to a boy, he was mad with happiness. He told all his friends about it and kept imagining what his son would be like: strong, robust, smart, the best guy in the world. At last, the son was born and the happy father went to the maternity hospital. When they showed him a baby wrapped in a blanket, he was completely amazed. "This little one is my son?!" "And what did you expect?" the nurse asked. "You thought he would have a high school diploma in his hands?"

Mysterious Discourses

49. Only after untying the boat from the dock,
   can you put out to sea.
Only after tearing the heart from the vain world,
   can you enter Eternal Life.

50. He who wakes up at dawn
   may feel the joy of a spring morning.
He who encounters the Truth
   may feel the joy of endless life.

51. When you recognize false friends,
   a real friend will appear.
When you discern the falsehood of thoughts,
   you will find inside of you a true foundation in life.

52. Teenagers were watching an action movie in a cinema and sharing their impressions out loud. People sitting near were asking them not to make noise. They kept apologizing but, carried away by the movie, kept forgetting their promises. An usher came up to them and said, "Boys, please stop talking." "But we are not talking, we are just thinking out loud," they replied. "If you wish to think out loud, do it outside," the usher said. "And in here keep silent, please."

53. If you stopped but a kilometer short of the city,
   this means you have not been there.
If you stopped but a step short of the summit,
   this means you have not conquered it.
If you stopped but a hair short of the drowning man,
   this means you have not saved him.
If but a single bad thought lives in your heart,
   this means you are still far from the Truth.

54. Start one chain saw in a quiet forest,
   and the entire forest will be filled with noise.

Harbor one unkind thought in your heart,
   and the entire world will seem unkind.

55. Do not think that the danger is distant,
   it is nearer than you think.
You believe that your enemy is a man,
   but your real enemy thinks you are an animal.
In order for him to see the man in you, conquer him now,
   otherwise, he will enslave you forever.

56. If you are visiting someone, the host first meets you at the door,
   and then takes you to the living room.
If you climb a mountain range,
   look for a village not upon the pass itself, but in the valley.
If you come to the limits of your knowledge, this is not the end yet,
   the Truth is much further.

57. If there is *that* in your perception,
   it is still not quite *that*.
If there is *this* in your perception,
   it is still not quite *this*.
If you have perceived *not that* and *not this*,
   it is still not quite *not that* and *not this*.

58. When you go outside the city boundaries,
   you see how spacious the earth is.
When you lean over a mountain precipice,
   you are surprised by its depth.
When the heart is cleared of bad thoughts,
   you are amazed by its immensity.

59. Do not expect anything good:
If a teenager begins to keep bad company.
If a man listens to what bad thoughts suggest to him.

60. A teenage gang attacked a boy who was returning home from school late in the evening. They robbed him of his money, beat him and left him in the street. A neighbor saw the boy lying unconscious and called his father. The father rushed to the place, took the boy in his arms and started carrying him home. But the boy came

to his senses and, thinking himself to be still in the hands of the attackers, screamed, "Let me go!" The father tried to calm him down but, in the dark, the boy was engulfed in fear and continued to cry and to try to break loose. Then the father carried the boy to a well-lit spot and told him, "My dear, this is me, your Dad. There is no one else here, just the two of us." The boy recognized his father, calmed down and whispered, "Dad, I love you more than anyone in the world."

61. Three people met: a man from the past, a man from the present and a man from the future. The man from the present asked the man from the past, "Take me with you to the past, I would very much like to see it." He replied, "If I take you to the past, you will not be able to live in the present anymore." Then the man from the present addressed the man from the future, "Take me along to the future." "If you see the future," he replied, "you will not be able to live in the present anymore." "Why are you giving me the same answer, although you are from different times?" the man from the present asked. "If you see the past, in comparison to it, the present will appear completely dark to you. You will get disappointed in the present and will not want to live in it anymore," the man from the past said with sympathy. "Then you, guest from the future, please explain to me why you do not want to show me your time," the man from the present asked? "If I show you the future," he replied with great sorrow, "A horrible sight will appear before you. You will despair and will also be unable to live in the present." "Well, in this case I better stay in my time," the man from the present sighed. "As of now, I can live in it."

62. All of a sudden, a boy started to behave strangely. He was sitting on the sofa silently and looking unceasingly at the clock. The alarmed parents came up to him, "Maybe you want some candy?" "No, I don't." "Maybe some chocolate?" "No." "Maybe a piece of cake?" "No." "What about ice cream?" "No," the boy replied with a heavy sigh and glanced at the clock impatiently. Suddenly, he jumped up with a cry of joy, "Hurrah! I've won! And now give me all you were offering me!" "But what happened?" the parents asked. "I made a bet with the guys that I would hold out for fifteen minutes, refusing everything that you offer me. And I bettered the previous result by five minutes!"

63. Fuss appears by itself. It engenders feverish activity and man loses himself.
Calm is a goal hard to attain but only in it the perception of the Truth is born and man finds himself, at last.

64. A blind man constantly asks, "Where am I?" in order to know his location. So you should also constantly ask yourself where you are,
   among good thoughts or bad ones.

65. A baby turns away from unfamiliar people and starts to cry when they try to take him in their arms. But he calms down at once when his mother clasps him to her bosom.
So, a morally clean soul does not accept false teachings but turns away from them at once and chooses but one —Word of Truth.

66. Where attention begins, purification begins.
Where purification begins, ascent begins.
Where ascent begins, perception begins.
Where perception begins, true Freedom is gained.

67. In a kingdom there lived a blacksmith. He learned to make chains so beautiful that he began to wear them on himself. Other blacksmiths liked the novelty. Then many other people started to put on chains and even the king and the aristocracy did it. The king issued a special decree on the universal wearing of chains. In schools, children were taught how to wear chains correctly. Jewelers began to make gold chains, silver chains and diamond-encrusted chains. Chains became the highest state award. There appeared skilled craftsmen making new and improved chains out of ultra light alloys. Scientific conferences and symposiums on chains were taking place. Scientists wrote a new version of the history of their kingdom. It proved that chains had been worn from extreme antiquity. Still, there appeared people who did not want to wear chains. They were subjected to persecution and imprisonment. As a punishment, special chains causing distress were placed upon them. However, on the threshold of death, they left a simple testament to the people, "Free yourselves from chains!" Gradually, there were more and more people who believed that testament. Some people took all the chains off, others just some of the chains. Those who liberated themselves explained to all that it became much easier for them to live. But the people just shook their heads distrustfully. "To be unlike the others is not the way for everyone," they would say and drift apart, jingling their chains. As time went by, the majority of the populace came to firmly realize that life without chains was actually possible. Then the king issued a new decree rehabilitating those who had suffered for the refusal to wear chains. A holiday was even established in honor of

the sufferers, but most still could not resolve to take off their chains, as they had grown accustomed to them.

68. A teenager asked his father, "Dad, what should I be like in life: strong or smart?" "It would be better if you are like bread and butter," the father answered. "I don't understand what you mean," the boy said. "In your actions be kind and soft as butter and in your intentions be simple and wise as bread," the father explained. "Then you will be useful to all."

69. The mother gave her son a key to the house and warned him that he would not be able to get in if he lost it. For a while, the boy was very cautious with regards to the key and always had it with him. But once, due to absent-mindedness, he lost it. The mother gave the boy the reserve key and said, "Son, make sure you don't lose this key; otherwise, we shall have extra problems. We'll either have to make a new key or to change the lock." "Mom, if I lose the second key too, I'll be able to get into the house through the window," the boy said. "No, no, my dear," the mother objected. "Don't make this a habit. People who don't know you may take you for a thief and call the police. It would actually be better if we make more reserve keys."

70. Do not look for the knowledgeable,
    look for the unknowledgeable, and you will know.
Do not live with the dead,
    die with the living, and you will live.

71. If you cut tree after tree,
    there will be nothing left even of a primeval forest.
If you catch fish with nets,
    even a sea will be emptied.
If you unceasingly destroy thought after thought,
    even a stubborn heart can be purified.

72. As long as there is wood in the fireplace,
    it will not stop burning.
As long as there are bad thoughts in the heart,
    it will not stop suffering.

73. Some villagers fell into the hands of a big gang of bandits. They took the villagers to their hideout in the mountains and forced them to work for the gang. The chief of the bandits grimly told the captives that he who would try to come out of the cave would be killed on the spot. The villagers, frightened by the threat, obeyed the order submissively. Even when the bandits went away to rob, the captives did not leave the cave. Once, a hunter who was passing by chanced upon them. He saw that the peasants were sorrowful and asked them what the matter was. The captives told him that they were enslaved by the bandits and were forbidden to exit the cave under the threat of death. The hunter was surprised and told the captives, "But the bandits are not here right now, why are you not running away?" "But they will kill us on the spot if they catch us!" the villagers replied fearfully. "I shall lead you away from here and the bandits will not be able to catch any one. Do you agree?" the hunter asked. The peasants exchanged glances and replied together, "We agree! Let us run away, before they return!" So they escaped together with the hunter and the bandits were not able to catch them.

74. A tourist bus approached a road sign that said, "Detour. Road repair." The driver turned off the highway and started moving cautiously along a temporary dirt road. The bus was going slowly, bypassing numerous potholes and rattling over the bumps. The guide told the driver, "The tourists are starting to worry. They are upset because we are going so slowly. I tried my best to distract them but they are not listening to me. They want you to take a good road." "Of course, I also want to take a good road but if the good road ended, where am I going to find it?" the driver replied. The guide took the microphone again and announced, "Dear guests! As soon as we reach a good road, we shall let you know right away." "As soon as we reach a good road, please let us rest," tired voices sounded.

75. A father had to use powerful pest-killers in his apple orchard. The grandfather, who was ill and resting in an armchair saw through the window of the house that his little grandson had plucked a very big and beautiful apple and was getting ready to eat it. "Grandson, don't eat that apple. It is very poisonous now!" the grandfather shouted to him through the window. "I have already wiped it with my sleeve," the boy replied. "Come closer, dear," the grandfather asked. When the boy came up to the window with the apple in his hand, the grandfather told him, "Listen to me. Don't eat the apple. Throw it away!" "It is very difficult for me to give it up right away," the boy said tearfully. "And would you be able to give it up gradually?" the

grandfather asked. "I don't know. I guess I could," the boy responded hesitantly. "Okay, take my pocket knife, cut the apple in two and throw one half of it away." The grandson did it. Then the grandfather asked the boy again, "What about the second half of the apple? Can you give it up?" "No. It would pain me." "Then cut the remaining half in two and throw one piece away." When the grandson fulfilled that request also, the grandfather asked him again, "And can you give up the quarter of the apple that remains?" "Sure, there is nothing left to eat." "So throw out what is left," the grandfather said. The boy followed his advice and said, surprised, "Granddad! Nothing remains of the apple now!" "Health remains, grandson! And also, you triumphed over yourself and that is more important than the apple. Wait for two or three weeks and we shall all eat our apples together."

76. A sincere and hopeful youth came to an elder and asked him only one question, "Elder, how can I be saved?" "Destroy your enemies," the reply came. "But I have never had any enemies," the youth said. Then the elder took him by the hand, led him afield and said, "Look for yourself." The young man saw a grand army covering the terrain up to the horizon. Shuddering with fear, he asked, "But what are those?" "Those are the false thoughts and ideas that you have accumulated in the course of your short life," the elder explained. "And who commands this terrible army?" "Your self-importance." "But how can I resist these innumerable hordes alone?" "Renounce your self-importance," the elder replied, "And all the enemies will run away from you."

77. To go away from the Truth is impossible,
    and to reach It is hard.
To go away from yourself is impossible,
    and to renounce yourself is hard.

78. A pack of wolves afield in the winter is not as dangerous to man
    as the angry thoughts that assail him.
A shoal of sharks at sea surrounding a drowning man is not as ferocious
    as the angry thoughts straying about him.

79. A drunkard will never get rid of tormenting thoughts with the help of wine.
A man who consents to bad thoughts will never think through all the evil that they
    sow in him.

80. Great is the joy of the man who survived a shipwreck, swam to shore and felt ground under his feet.
But incomparable is the joy of the man who, amid the bitter and boundless sea of sorrows, discovered the indestructible refuge, the rock of Truth with a never-ending source of Living Water

81. Fantasies that man builds up
   often seem beautiful to him.
But the life that is built in accordance with those fantasies
   turns out terrible.

82. A farmer's neighbor came to see him. The farmer's family members told him that he had stepped outside to look at something in the yard. The neighbor walked across the entire yard but failed to find the farmer. He saw some workers passing by and asked them where their employer could be. They advised him to go to the garden. The neighbor walked across the entire garden but did not see his friend anywhere and decided to call out his name. The host responded from the vineyard and came out to meet the guest at once. "Friend, I have not been able to find you anywhere until you responded," the neighbor said. "And you will never be able to find me here until I come out to you myself," the farmer said. "If you had called me right away, I would have responded right away and no search would have been necessary."

83. A motorist came to a strange city where there were several dozen traffic lights at every intersection. The strangest thing was that they were all working without coordination. But the residents somehow were driving in their cars without hitting each other. The driver felt lost and parked at the side of the road. He noticed a pedestrian and asked him through his car window, "Could you tell me why you have so many traffic lights?" "We heard that it was a very useful thing, so we put them everywhere, the more the better," the pedestrian replied. "But how is one to follow their signals?" "No one follows their signals here. All the drivers give signs to each other." "And what is the most common sign of your drivers?" the puzzled newcomer asked. "Pointing a finger at their temple," the pedestrian grinned.

84. A rumor reached the beasts that somewhere in the world there lived a Sun Hare.* Those who were more timid grew alarmed. Maybe that strange animal could bring some trouble? The carnivorous beasts, being more daring, began to say that the Sun

Hare should be caught and eaten, so that it did not exist anymore. "This way, everyone will be safer," they were assured. The sharpest and the most inquisitive of the beasts suggested starting a search for the Sun Hare right away. "Possibly, it is an animal of cosmic origin and it will convey to us its unique knowledge," they supposed and asked the council of the beasts for extra food supplies for the participants of an expedition. Even the lions felt uneasy, "And what if this Sun Hare wants to usurp power?" They decreed, "The Sun Hare is hereby pronounced an instigator of disturbances and, should it be found somewhere, it is to be apprehended and jailed." There also appeared a quiet uncommon opinion that the Sun Hare was elusive and completely out of reach. And the skeptical minded among the beasts repudiated everything and claimed that all the theories about the Sun Hare were but fables created by earthworms for their consolation. Finally, the council of the beasts ordered the snails, the most unhurried and meticulous researchers, to study the matter and prepare a survey of it. Up until now, the beasts have been waiting for that survey.
(*In Russian, "Sun Hare" (солнечный зайчик) is the common name for a spot of reflected light usually produced by children with the help of a pocket mirror.)

85. It is easy to be healthy,
   but it is very hard to recover health.
Perception of the Truth is simple,
   but to keep hold of It is not within everyone's strength.

86. A master cabinetmaker made splendid furniture and had many customers. Once, he heard people say that his models were out of date and did not look modern enough. The cabinetmaker switched to newer models but some of his customers considered them somewhat outdated as well. The man began to use the most advanced materials but people were buying his furniture less and less, saying that it still did not correspond to modern demands. The cabinetmaker began to create authentic models but, to his surprise, heard from the clients that he was behind the times. Now retro furniture was in, made of real wood! The disappointed cabinetmaker complained to one of his old customers, "As much as I try, people cannot be pleased." "You should not have followed your clients' whims," the friend replied. "That way, you forgot how to make old furniture and have not learned to make the new."

87. The earthly sun rises in any weather, regardless of the storms and tempests. And the unearthly Sun prefers silence and rises in man's heart, akin to a light breeze.

88. A man suddenly woke up and realized that he was in a boat being carried away by a rapid river current. To the right and to the left of him were slippery rocks and there was nothing to cling to. The boat was being carried downstream, towards a roaring waterfall. The man realized that it remained to him only to start rowing with all his might against the current. There was still hope to row out of the narrow gorge and reach the bank. It was clear. If he were to start analyzing how he got into this predicament, he would perish before he could understand anything. The man pulled a good oar and the boat began to slowly move away from the terrible waterfall. The man felt that his strength was almost over but suddenly, to his great joy, he saw behind a rock a man who threw a rope to him and helped him to land.

89. A fledgling asked its mother, the seagull, "How can I learn to fly?" "Flap your wings unceasingly all the time and you will fly," the seagull responded. "But I am still unable to take flight. I keep falling down and grow tired," the fledgling objected. "That is okay. Just don't despair and believe what I have told you," the seagull reassured the fledgling. "When your wings become a bit stronger, you will fly. It will come to you naturally."

90. A seeker of Truth heard that somewhere far away in the mountains there lived a wise man. He was looking for that wise man for a long time but was still unable to find him. Eventually growing tired of the long way, the man sat down by a clear mountain spring and considered already ending his quest. At that moment, he saw a child playing with flowers in a glade. Surprised by the unexpected encounter, the seeker asked the child, "Who are you and where have you come from?" But the child said nothing and only smiled. With a trusting smile he extended to the seeker of Truth a flower. He took it in his hand and at that very instant saw himself as an infant, the way he was in distant childhood, then as a youth, then as a mature man, surrounded by his family, then as an ill and weak old man. He saw his demise and, finally, even his grave. When the seeker came to his senses, there was no one at the glade but him. Then he made a shelter out of branches at that spot and stayed there. The seeker of Truth never learned whom he had met at the glade. And when people came to him, he smiled and silently gave them flowers.

Mysterious Discourses

91. He who goes in pursuit of his desires again and again is like a man who goes deeper and deeper into the dark forest and finds his perdition there.
He who refuses to fulfill his desires again and again is like a man who gradually emerges from a dark thicket towards the sun and the light and finds his salvation there.

92. A house without tenants is not alive.
A heart that does not live the Eternal Life is dead.

93. They are close to ruin:
The man who is drowning in icy water,
The heart that is drowning in the icy water of bad thoughts.
The ship that sprang a big leak,
The heart into which bad thoughts flow freely.

94. A traveler who had seen a lot in his life was asked, "What is the most amazing country that you have visited?" "The country where people entombed themselves alive," he replied with deep sorrow. They asked him to tell them more about that country. "Over there, people bury themselves alive in crypts. The richer ones entomb themselves in gold and silver crypts and the poorer ones in crypts made out of colored stones or even simple cobblestones, but the crypts are well constructed. All of the awards and medals that they receive in their lifetime bear the images of their mausoleums. They all die there in terrible torment but the residents of that country try not to think too much about it." "Maybe one should explain to them that they act irrationally?" "That is impossible," the traveler said sadly. "They believe that this is precisely the meaning of their life."

95. Two friends got lost in the mountains late at night. They switched on their flashlights and unexpectedly came to a large cave. It started to rain, so they made a campfire and began to settle down for the night. One of the men walked a little deeper into the cave and, seeing that it was very deep, told his friend, "Listen. Let's study the cave to the end. It's very interesting." "But it's nighttime," the other friend objected. "Let us go there after dawn." "But in a deep cave it makes no difference if it is day or night. It does not matter." "Actually, that's right," the second man said. So they started walking towards the heart of the cave. Soon, the last gleams of the campfire remained far behind. The friends stopped and turned off their flashlights.

There was absolute darkness around them. "Such darkness," one of the friends whispered. "Yes, but it is not like regular darkness. It is light somehow," the other one responded, also in a whisper. "You can even listen to it."

96. There lived two friends. One of them stuttered and the other was hard of hearing. They learned that a new method of curing stuttering and deafness had appeared and decided to take advantage of it. In a while, after successful treatment, the friends met and were very happy to see each other. "H-h-how are you doing?" the first friend asked. "What? Say it again?" the other friend replied. "You d-d-don't h-h-hear well?" "No, I hear well, I just got used to asking others to repeat. And why are you stuttering?" "I also g-g-got used to it."

97. When a man climbs a mountain pass,
   he cannot help but be astonished by the magnificence of the landscape.
When a man purifies his heart,
   he cannot help but be amazed by what he sees in its innermost depth.

98. If rubbish is cleared from the house, but dust remains,
   that is not cleaning yet.
If lust and anger are killed in you, but unkind thoughts still remain in your heart,
   that is not yet the pureness God wants from you.

99. Don't miss the target,
   kill unkind thoughts before they kill you.
Don't fight against men,
   kill your vanity before it kills you.

100. A young man who lived in a house by a river heard from the people about the Good King and wanted to see him very much. Once they knocked at his gate. He came outside and saw a royal servant who told him, "The king found out that you wanted to see him but, for your desire to be fulfilled, you must pass several trials." "But what are they?" "You will see on your way," the messenger smiled mysteriously and departed. The young man took some money and food, locked the house and set off. On the way, he met a beggar woman who was entreating him to help her. He shared what he could with her but the beggar woman insisted that he should give her all the money he had on him and the bag with food. "Otherwise you will not get to

the king," she added. The young man gave her all she was asking for and went ahead. Soon he saw a running crowd of frightened peasants. They were shouting that the riverside villages were being flooded and that he had to run to save his property. The youth decided to return to his house but one of the men running past him suddenly exclaimed, "But what about the king?" Those words set the young man to venture with resolution; so, he continued on his way.

Then the youth saw a sick man by the road who was moaning pitifully, "Help me, good fellow." "But how can I help you?" the youth asked. "Take my illness upon yourself, then I shall live some more in the wide world. I need to raise my children and to support my elderly parents. Without me, they are lost." "But if I fall ill, how will I be able to reach the king?" the young man thought. But then he remembered the words of the royal servant about the trials awaiting him on the way and replied, "I agree. I will take your illness upon myself." At that very instant, he became sick and the cured man went home, rejoicing over his recovery.

Finally, the young man, ill and exhausted, without food or money, living entirely on alms, reached the royal palace. The very servant who had come to his house met him. "On your way, you did everything right," he praised the young man. "All of the people you helped were royal servants and therefore I am happy to greet you here. For the time being, fortify yourself with the food that the king has sent for you." After tasting the royal fare, the youth recovered right away. "And now I shall at last see the king?" he asked. "You fulfilled all the conditions set by the king," the servant replied. "But it is the king's own decision whom and when to receive at the palace. So await the royal decision here. That is the final trial."

Conclusion
Eternal Life

Do not pursue what is leaving you.
Do not push away what comes on its own.
Know that there is no true happiness either in the one, or in the other.

1. A hermit who was living in the woods once dreamed of acquiring some miraculous abilities. He intensified his ascetic exploits and received the ability to cure all illnesses and to resurrect the dead. But he wanted more. The hermit further intensified his ascetic struggle and received clairvoyance. He knew all about every man and every event in the world. The hermit's interest towards miraculous abilities grew further and he kept multiplying his ascetic feats. He received the ability to fly and to become invisible. "I wonder what is next," the hermit thought. His ascetic zeal seemed to know no limits. But then he suddenly felt that all of his miraculous abilities vanished and he was again the way he had been before. "The same again?" thought the amazed hermit. And he heard a voice, "Yes, the same. Because you do not know how to use even that."

2. If you do not know what the Truth is,
   it pains you to lose even a hair of your head.
If you know the Truth, the way It is,
   it does not pain you to lose even your life for Its sake.

3. You will never meet Eternity in a crowd,
   It prefers seclusion.

But you should never prefer seclusion,
   to Eternity.

Mysterious Discourses

4. Do not pursue what is leaving you.
Do not push away what comes on its own.
Know that there is no true happiness either in the one, or in the other.

5. A child is swinging on a swing. Then he sees his parents, jumps off the swing and runs to meet them. And the swing gradually slows down and stops.

A man is ringing a bell and the sound of the chimes goes far into the distance. Now he strikes the bell for the last time and descends from the belfry. And the sound is still flowing in the air, gradually vanishing afar.

6. Arm yourself with patience and safeguard yourself with what you have understood. A time will come when what you have understood will strengthen and become transformed inside of you into a new life. You do not know it yet but it belonged to you from the beginning.

7. All dreams, thoughts and desires exist only in what begins and ends. Not one dream, not one thought, not one desire can penetrate beyond that limit. There abides a new Life that has no end.

8. A man lived in Fantasy City on Fantasy Street. His job was fantastic and his salary too. He had a fantastic family and was creating the most fantastic fantasies about his fantastic life. As all the citizens of Fantasy where fantasizing, their life was fantastically difficult. So the man from Fantasy Street, seeing the constant failures of his fantastic plans, decided to find the greatest fantasy of all, with the help of which he could improve his fantastic affairs.

On the street, he chanced upon a traveler from a distant land and realized that he was not one of his fantasizing fellow citizens. "Excuse me, I see that you are not from amongst the fantasizing," he addressed the traveler. "Could you advise me what I am to do? Help me to set my fantasies straight and to find the main fantasy of my life that I must hold onto." "Yes, you are right, I am not of the fantasizing," the traveler replied. "And here is my advice to you. Stop the quest for the main fantasy. Simply stop fantasizing. And then you will understand what you are to do and your entire life will cease being a fantasy right away." "But if I no longer fantasize, how will I be able to live among the fantasizing?" "How? You will see," the traveler said and took off.

9. The best hearing is hearing nothing.
The best tale is silence.
The best knowledge is obliviousness to all knowledge.
The best vision is Revelation.

10. If something had been otherwise,
   nothing would have been.
The Truth cannot be other,
   because in that case, It would never have been the Truth.
It is everlastingly
   the way It is.

11. You may come to the Truth when you are not going anywhere.
You may hear It when you are not hearing anything.
You may see It when you are not seeing anything.
You may learn It when you are not learning anything.

12. The disciples asked the hermit to leave a testament that would give them the key to what he had comprehended. The hermit bequeathed to his disciples a book in which he wrote about himself but asked to have it read only after his death. That time had come. The hermit died and was interred by his disciples. They came to his hut and took the book left for them by their master. Opening it, they read his testament, "I am the greatest fool, forgive me!" There was nothing else in the book.

Epilogue
Spring

Spring comes and the earth gets covered with flowers.
Time comes and new life awakes in the heart.

***

Forget everything you have read in this book and its meaning will be revealed to you.

www.ingramcontent.com/pod-product-compliance
Lightning Source LLC
Chambersburg PA
CBHW022227010526
44113CB00033B/645